THE CONSCIOUS PARENTING HANDBOOK

Spines

THE CONSCIOUS PARENTING HANDBOOK

365 Conscious parenting posts, tips, and therapeutic play activities

JAY MORGAN, LPE

with

HANNAH MORGAN, LPC

The Conscious Parenting Handbook is dedicated to parents (and other adults) who know there is something better, who are tired of feeling stuck, and who are sick of saying and doing the same old things. This book is for the reader who earnestly desires, not only to better their parenting but to transform it...

CONTENTS

A YEAR OF WISDOM

A review of 'The Conscious Parenting Handbook,' by Diana Ganea, a conscious mom, an educator, and a friend.

The Conscious Parenting Handbook breaks away and diverges from conventional books on parenting. Instead of lengthy chapters, *The Handbook* offers wisdom in bite-sized pieces. There are daily posts on Conscious Parenting, thought-provoking information on child psychology, personal reflections, and some down-to-earth, practical advice on how to work with children. Interestingly, all of this is presented within a 365-day calendar format. Early in the book, Mr, Morgan writes, "A Conscious Parenting post a day keeps unconscious parenting away." It is the author's belief that taking in regular information on Conscious Parenting makes it much harder, and eventually impossible, to stay trapped in the dark domain of unconscious parenting.

The Conscious Parenting Handbook delves into the complex world of parenting as seen through the lens of opposites—conscious versus unconscious behavior. It offers many useful insights that go well beyond superficial analysis. Mr. Morgan emphasizes the importance of understanding both the conscious, and unconscious mind so we can avoid strong emotional reactions—reactions that often have their roots in our own upbringing, and past experiences. The first chapters, as well as the daily snippets, offer guidance on recognizing these unconscious patterns, as well as ways to break free from them. Most importantly, there are guideposts to help parents connect with their children from a place of love—not just the love of the ego, but higher self-love. This kind of love results in a more authentic relationship with our children and allows us to be more conscious and present in our daily lives.

The Conscious Parenting Handbook offers a unique blend of spontaneity and predictability. Daily posts on various topics are inserted in a seemingly random order, mimicking the unpredictable nature of parenthood. However, *The Handbook* also offers a sense of structure through recurring segments like "Why not try this?" which describe fun activities and actionable tips. Others like "Psych 101" provide simple and many times entertaining explanations of sometimes hard to grasp psychological concepts.

Mr. Morgan's light-hearted approach and real-life experiences add a layer of warmth and relatability. It reminds the reader that they are not alone in this intricate, and sometimes baffling world of parenting. Mr. Morgan becomes an ally, guiding the reader into an awakened mindset where parenting is simple again and, yes, fun.

PROLOGUE

Hi. My name is Jay Morgan. As I jokingly like to say, "All I've ever done in my life is deliver newspapers, wait tables, and help children and families." (Of course, I'm exaggerating, but not much.)

Now that I'm approaching the end of my career, I want to help others by sharing what I have learned and, more often than not, what children have taught me. My daughter, Hannah, has made her own contributions and has helped me with structuring the book and editing.

The Conscious Parenting Handbook has at least one Conscious Parenting post for every day of the year. But, *The Handbook* is not just a one-year calendar—it's an every-year calendar. The generic format allows the reader to go through the daily posts again and again, no matter what year it is. And since it's a book, it's portable. As parents, we can't afford to leave Conscious Parenting on the shelf; we have to take it with us.

The Handbook also contains some informal case studies, pulled from my work with children, along with some compelling information on child psychology that will bring this often underappreciated science to life.

Finally, there are many therapeutic activities where kids will learn and have fun, all at the same time.

And, if one post a day isn't enough, you can always read *The Conscious Parenting Handbook* from beginning to end. I suggest rereading important posts to fully digest their meaning. Or why not open the book to a random page? There might be a Conscious Parenting post waiting there, just right for the moment at hand.

So, let's get to it…

INTRODUCTION

Unconsciousness has a tremendous hold on us. To complicate things, we are usually unaware of the many ways that our unconscious "choices" impact our lives. When we behave unconsciously, it's so automatic that we are not aware we are behaving unconsciously. When this happens, unconscious determinants control us. We have no real freedom.

So, unconsciousness can be seen as both an affliction and the human condition. But for many, unconsciousness is the norm. "This is just how I am. It's how I've always been," some people say. The message here is that other people must somehow step up, and learn to deal with an unconscious person's behavior (which, interestingly, we can do, but only by becoming more conscious ourselves).

In the counseling business, we say that people can't work on a problem until they admit that they have one. Until then, they are, in a way, sleepwalking—oblivious of how their unconscious behavior affects themselves and others. Or, they may get glimpses of their unconscious behavior but have become, to some degree, comfortable with it. Or, maybe a person is uncomfortable with it, but they are not ready, or don't know how to change. In each of the above cases, the starting point is the same: We must realize that we often behave unconsciously and that unconscious behavior messes things up and holds us back. Unconsciousness can also damage relationships and our overall quality of life.

Since unconsciousness is so deep within us, we must take somewhat drastic measures to counteract it, not in a fearful way, but in a determined way. Typically, this involves engaging in activities that help us: 1) break away from compulsive thinking (reflection, meditation, mindfulness training, etc.) and 2) be more in touch with our bodies (yoga, inner bodywork, progressive relaxation, etc.)

It is also very helpful (and mandatory for some, including myself) to read spiritual texts and listen to spiritual talks. The reasoning here is simple: we read or listen to someone who is at a high level of consciousness, and they describe and point the way to a higher level of consciousness that we, too, can begin to enjoy.

As we take in this new information, the power-packed messages begin to chip away at our old conditioned ways of thinking and behaving. We are then able to finally break free from long-standing, unconscious influences. We become more of the parent (and person) we always wanted to be. I believe *The Conscious Parenting Handbook* will be a big help in this process.

UNCONSCIOUS PARENTING VERSUS CONSCIOUS PARENTING

Conscious Parenting and Unconscious Parenting are polar opposites. Let's take a brief look at some of the key differences between the two.

Unconscious Parenting is when we reflexively say and do the first thing that comes into our mind. This process is almost always driven by feelings. These can be feelings from the past that we suppressed or the feelings we experience in the now moment.

Unconscious parenting can also be an old, conditioned behavior pattern or communication style that was imposed on us when we were young (sometimes called a "psychodrama"). As parents, we then take these ingrained patterns and play them forward, bringing them into our own families and directing them at those we love. This is almost always an unconscious process. Examples would include criticism, relentless teasing, labeling, sarcasm, shaming, and "not good enough" comments, just to name a few.

In contrast, **Conscious Parenting** is the ability to notice in our mind what we want to say and do, but taking the time to make sure that what we want to say and do is a good idea, to make sure it has a therapeutic value, and will do no harm. It is not an emotional reaction or an old, ingrained style of interacting.

Conscious Parenting is always fresh and new. And, it is not arrived at solely through thinking but through intuition, higher-self knowledge and the compassion we have for another.

Conscious Parenting is vital to the health and well-being of our children and families. It is a gift that lasts a lifetime. And the personal benefits? They are immense.

 *With Conscious Parenting, children and parents grow up together."*

— JAY MORGAN

LOVE AND A HARD TRUTH

Love is the foundation of Conscious Parenting and the starting point. When in doubt, love.

But what keeps us from loving the way we want? Why do we so often fall short?

The author, Dean Koontz, once made an interesting observation. He wrote that people are all "the walking wounded."

The Walking Wounded? What?!?! That's a very uncomfortable thought! Not a great way to start a book. And a surefire way to turn off some readers.

But other readers? They know all too well the truth of this statement. And many readers may sense the truth behind these words and be curious enough to read on...

All of us, unknowingly, accumulate emotional pain. This pain can be created by the mean words and selfish behavior of unconscious people, or we can absorb it from others throughout the day.

But, believe it or not, our compulsive, non-stop thinking generates most of our emotional pain. We don't control our thinking—in a very real way, our thinking controls us. In our mind, a sad thought generates a sad feeling, an angry thought generates an angry feeling, a nervous thought, a nervous feeling, and so on. This mind-made emotional pain then turns into a type of negative energy that becomes lodged in our psyche (or inner self). This energy can affect our mood, our behavior, our body, and even our health.

Emotional pain also keeps us psychologically closed. If someone tried to stick their finger in your eye, your eye would automatically close to protect itself. When we feel emotionally threatened (a very uncomfortable feeling arises in our conscious awareness), our psyche does the same thing: it closes to what it perceives as a threat. Over time, with continued stress, the psyche just stays closed. It will become partially closed, mostly closed, or it can even become completely closed.

A person's closedness fluctuates, depending on one's degree of woundedness and the situation at hand. Being closed leads to many unconscious behaviors and is the natural result of woundedness. When we become closed, our feelings begin to harden. This unconscious process becomes a twisted trade-off: As our feelings harden, we don't feel as much emotional pain, but, at the same time, it becomes virtually impossible for us to give and receive love. We also become less aware of, and less concerned with, how our behavior affects other people. We unknowingly go into a type of self, or more accurately, ego-preservation mode.

Sadly, if we parents don't heal from our past woundedness, we will unintentionally inflict wounds on our children ("Hurt people hurt people"). Or, we just won't be all that we need to be for them.

The fix? Psychological healing and spiritual practice. We will touch on this, but see my other book, *The Little Book of Sutras,* for more.

So, let's summarize. To truly love our children and other people, we must: 1) create the conscious intention (or plan) to love, 2) develop enough self-awareness and discipline to not act on harmful emotional impulses—impulses that would push us into saying and doing things that are unloving, and 3) devote ourselves to personal growth and healing.

Oh, yes. There is one more thing. Love can originate from the egoic self, or love can be almost effortlessly channeled by the higher self. Egoic love is great—a solid starting point. But the ultimate goal is to channel loving words and actions, which are "gifts" from our higher self.

The entire Koontz quote is interesting, and definitely deserving of a closer look…

> *We are all the walking wounded in a world that is a war zone. Everything we love will be taken from us, everything, last of all, life itself. Yet everywhere I look, I find great beauty in this battlefield, and grace, and the promise of joy."*

Koontz reminds us that, regardless of our life situation, beauty and grace are always there, waiting to be discovered. And, in my experience, joy occurs naturally, to the degree we escape compulsive thought. Joy bubbles up from inside us and is not dependent on any set of outer circumstances.

But is the world really a battlefield? It can be. If a person comes to see the world as a battlefield, they will be inclined to argue and fight. Angry thinking will consume them, and angry feelings will fill them up. Over time, what they think becomes their reality. Angry thinking has locked them in a battle with people and forces outside themselves. Their thinking has trapped them in their own personal hell.

Practically everyone would agree that the world is difficult and that life can be painful. But these difficulties can also be seen as challenges, a set of opportunities for us to grow, evolve, and expand our conscious awareness. If life wasn't difficult, many people might not be interested and motivated to grow.

But, I have to disagree with Koontz on one important point: while our physical, mental, and emotional existence will be surrendered at the time of death, the spirit lives on. This part of us is eternal and is not subject to the limitations of our physical, mental and emotional existence.

Eckhart Tolle once said that many people think the opposite of life is death. But that's not really true. Tolle points out that people are born, they have a lifespan, and then they die. But their life, the energy that animates their bodies, is not subject to this cycle. If energy is neither created nor destroyed, our essence as a person—that which makes us alive—has always been here, and will always be here. And perhaps the best part is that this energy can be accessed, tapped into, and utilized in our daily lives…

And, while many people do live in a war zone, inside and outside their minds, others are opting for peace and transcendence. They are starting their inward journey, beginning to rise above the ego, and escape its destructive influence. This is not an easy journey, but it is possibly the most important journey of our lives.

Now, on to *The Conscious Parenting Handbook*—a perpetual, one-post-a-day calendar for this year and every year.

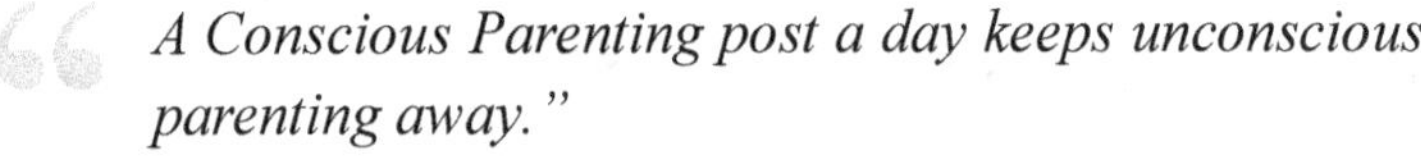

A Conscious Parenting post a day keeps unconscious parenting away."

— JAY MORGAN

JANUARY

1. Infants do not know who they are. How could they? At birth, a baby is a bundle of beingness—pure consciousness, interwoven into a tiny body. Young children "learn" who they are by the messages they receive from their parents and other caregivers. These messages can be spoken or unspoken, and they become the building blocks for a child's developing self-image. A child will literally "grow into" and become the messages we give them.

2. The most important message we can send to our children is that they are loved exactly the way they are. They don't have to do anything to earn love, and they can't do anything to lose it.

3. Grace is an undervalued but powerful Conscious Parenting tool. Showing grace is when a parent does not immediately give a misbehaving child what they think the child deserves.

Grace often creates an "Aha moment." A child messes up, but there's no reactive punishment. They are then more likely to think about their behavior, see how it was maladaptive, and maybe even notice how it made another person feel. Grace is patient, loving and a very powerful catalyst for change. And once grace is employed, a parent's response will be more compassionate and effective.

4. Loving others is your gift. To do it right, expect nothing in return. A parent's felt love, consciously expressed and received, helps children learn to love themselves.

Loving kids well doesn't happen by accident. Loving our children is an intentional, moment-by-moment choice. If we don't choose to act in a loving way, there's a good chance we will act in an unloving way.

5. Love is not like Skittles. We don't have to be afraid we will run out. With the ongoing and renewed intention to love, there will always be love to give and love to share. (*Caveat: Egoic love can run out as we "will ourselves" to love. And conflicted feelings will often sabotage our ability to love. But love from our higher self transcends conflicted feelings and is more enduring.*)

Why not try this? Elizabeth Barrett Browning said, *"How do I love thee? Let me count the ways."* Sit down with your kids and brainstorm all the ways we show each other love. Make sure they understand that we can do a nice thing begrudgingly (where our heart is not in it), or we can do something nice for someone as a way to show our love. (Extra credit: Then everyone gets to sing along with the song "Love Train" by the O'Jays, and hopefully, everyone will get on board!)

Added bonus: The first part of this activity is left-brain work, and the second part is right-brain play.

6.

> *How bold a child becomes when they are completely sure they are loved."*

— SIGMUND FREUD

7. A parent can become completely enamored with their children. But, if we're not careful, we can end up wrapped around someone's little finger, with their footprints up and down our back. We must rely on non-emotional reasoning to make sure our decisions are where they need to be. Even the love we feel for our children can sometimes be a stumbling block if we're not careful.

8. Love is the glue to any healthy relationship. When in doubt, love. Conscious Parenting is expanding on our ability to show love to our kids, regardless of how they are acting.

 *The moment you expect something, it's business, not love."*

— SWAMI PARTHASARATHY

9. Positive attention is proactive. Negative attention is reactive. Positive attention, done consistently, often keeps behavior problems from ever arising.

Case Study: Four-year-old Savannah never liked to be held or hugged. Her parents suspected it had something to do with her surgery the day after she was born, and the two weeks she spent on the neonatal intensive care unit. During this time, Savannah had needles and tubes going in and coming out of various parts of her body. While her dad held her, he held her nervously, worriedly, like he was afraid she might break. Now, at four, a touchy-feely person, Savannah was not.

Savannah's bedtime routine usually involved a peck on the cheek but nothing more. Dad wondered how he might help Savannah break the ice, and bring her into the wonderful world of hugging and cuddling. Then, one night, a conscious intervention came to him…

As Dad was tucking Savannah into bed, he told his daughter that his parents, Nana and Pepaw, didn't hug him much when he was a kid (which was true). Because of this, when Dad hugged someone, he said it felt "funny" and "weird" (also true). He asked if Savannah might help by giving Dad "hugging lessons." With bright eyes, Savannah sat up excitedly. *Dad helped her a lot, and now there was a way for Savannah to help him!* Savannah squeezed her dad tight, and Dad held her close. A moment passed. The ice began to melt…

10. Using negative strategies to change a child's behavior— lecturing, raising our voices, threatening, intimidation, and punishment—is like pushing a boulder uphill. And pushing a boulder uphill is the easiest of the two.

11. Conscious parents know that loving a child is not enough. Children must be able to feel a parent's love, take it in, and absorb it. But how do we do that?

The four major ways to relate felt love are 1) eye contact, 2) physical touch, 3) focused attention, and 4) positivity—positive feedback, encouragement, strategic compliments, and affirming statements. Don't leave this critical responsibility to chance. Make it your intention, and practice daily. Kids do best when they are "filled up" with a parent's love. This translates into a positive sense of self and, later, more feelings of self-love, along with the ability to better show love to others.

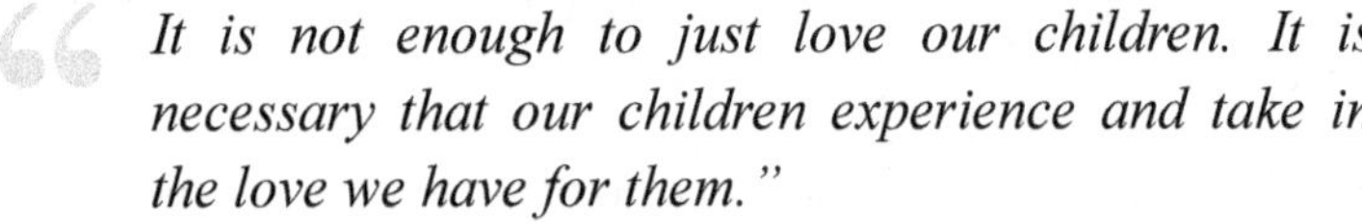

> *It is not enough to just love our children. It is necessary that our children experience and take in the love we have for them."*
>
> — JAY MORGAN

12. Logic suggests that we can't build a stable family without working on our own instability. When we approach a family member with stability, we are a real help to them. If we approach a family member with instability, we will not be much of a help, and tense moments may escalate and get worse.

13. Once we more clearly understand our child's specific psychology, we will see them and work with them in a completely different way. Until then, parents are often just working on a child's "bad behavior" or "poor attitude."

Psych 101: Feelings are neither good nor bad. Feelings are best described as "comfortable" or "uncomfortable."

If children believe that some feelings are "good" and some feelings are "bad," they will probably try to force the good feelings and cling to them. At the same time, they might try to avoid or push the bad ones away.

But if we teach children that feelings can be comfortable or uncomfortable, the uncomfortable ones start to seem less scary and easier to manage. Kids start to understand that, if they allow an uncomfortable feeling to be there, and if they allow themselves to feel it, the uncomfortable feeling will begin to move through. This process works the same with our thoughts, which can also be comfortable or uncomfortable.

14. If we had magic glasses that let us see the inner damage we cause when we are harsh and critical, it would be much easier to stop and to change.

15. When we are fully immersed in positive parenting—when we become fluid in our ability to notice positive behavior, improvement, and the absence of negative behavior—any constructive criticism we offer will be truly constructive and helpful. It will come from a completely different place inside us and cause little to no defensiveness and reactivity in a child.

16.

> *Anything that irritates us about a child's behavior can lead us to a deeper understanding of ourselves."*
>
> — ADAPTED FROM A QUOTE BY CARL JUNG

Why not try this? Here are two questions to ask ourselves when we feel irritation towards our child: "What is it about my child's behavior that is so irritating right now?" and "What is it about my thinking (or belief system) that is creating such strong irritation in me?"

Sometimes, parents think their child is TRYING to make them angry or upset. This belief will always cause a strong emotional reaction in the parent. In reality, most misbehavior is passive-aggressive, primarily unconscious behavior that springs from a child's emotional upsetness. If a parent reminds themself that their child carries around emotional pain, and this pain will sometimes "leak out of them" in the form of bad behavior, they will no longer take a child's negative behavior so personally. Then they can more consciously respond.

Other times, a parent reacts to a mental expectation—a picture the parent has in their mind of what a child's behavior "should be" at that moment. And when the child fails to meet that expectation, a parent reacts.

17. "Fast and Furious" may make for a good action movie, but not for a smoothly running and healthy family. Is all the busyness and hectic pace really necessary? Fast and Furious can morph into a lifestyle if we're not careful. It pushes us towards hurriedly doing things and with less attention. If we can do something quickly and efficiently, great. But we can't let this mindset creep into our interactions with our children. Busy and hectic parenting often devolves into haphazard and unconscious parenting.

> *In this modern world where activity is stressed almost to the point of mania, quietness as a childhood need is too often overlooked. Yet a child's need for quietness is the same today as it has always been—it may even be greater—for quietness is an essential part of all awareness. In quiet times and dreamy times, a child can dwell in thoughts of their own, and in songs, and stories of their own making."*

> — ADAPTED FROM A QUOTE BY MARGARET WISE BROWN

Many people busily skip over the surface of life. They seem unaware of the field of stillness and quietness that is superimposed onto the physical world, waiting in the background, beckoning us.

Other people notice this field but seem afraid because it is so different from their normal feeling state. But, only by discovering this field of stillness and quietness can a person reconnect with their true depth and discover the hidden riches inside them."

— JAY MORGAN

18. Parents should anticipate and meet a child's needs. But then there are their "wants."

"But I want it!" a child will say. Or, they will dig in their heels and say, "But *I don't want* to do that."

Kids must first learn to accept "No." Then, they have to get their wants met in a healthy way. Getting a want met in an unhealthy way (by manipulating, wearing a parent down, being sneaky, throwing a fit, etc.) leads to bad learning, and often the development of negative behavior patterns as a child gets older.

19. Strong-willed kids often get the wrong idea. They want to put you off, negotiate, compromise, or make a deal before they have mastered the task of simply following directions.

In baseball, remind your child that you have to run to first base before you can run to second. If a player runs to second base first, they're out. Let your child know you will be glad to be more flexible with them and make some special allowances when they demonstrate the ability to consistently "run to first base"—to be able to listen, and consistently follow your directions.

20. A basic premise in behavioral psychology is, "Any behavior that is rewarded is more likely to reoccur." With many children, this premise has to be modified to, "Any behavior that you 'make a fuss over' (or put energy into) is more likely to reoccur." Let's put our energy into our child's positive or improved behaviors—not their negative and unhealthy ones.

21. There is the "old stuff" and the "new stuff." The "old stuff" will, not surprisingly, bring the same old results. To make a place for the "new stuff," we have to practice what's called "not doing." This is the practice of not saying and not doing, the first thing that comes into our mind—intentionally not saying or doing the same old stuff. This makes room for the "new stuff" to enter our minds. The "new stuff" comes from pure awareness and creates new connections, fresh ideas, and novel approaches. This is the highest form of Conscious Parenting.

Why not try this? At least once a day, find a comfortable place to sit in stillness and silence. Close your eyes and look inward. There, you will begin to notice your impulses—the things you would've said, or the things you would've done if you had not been doing the exercise. (One time, when I was doing this exercise, I "found myself" in the kitchen, making a sandwich. I just smiled, shook my head, put the half-made sandwich in the fridge, and went back to my chair to finish my time.)

During this meditation, you will notice a thought to say something… but you don't say anything. You will also notice a thought to do something… but you don't do anything. You simply sit in stillness and watch your thoughts come, and then you watch your thoughts go.

Done regularly, this one practice will break up old, conditioned ways of parenting quicker than anything.

22. Along with compliments on specific behaviors, let's be sure to praise a perceived trend. Here's an example:

Behavior: "I love how you're getting along with your sister right now. You're sharing with her and taking turns."

Trend: "I've noticed you trying harder to get along with your sister. You are being much more patient with her and not aggravating her nearly as much. That's so great! Thank you!"

These kinds of messages consolidate gains and help a child get to the final step of positive change—internalizing a positive, prosocial behavior. Then, they will no longer need reminders or parental direction.

23. Multitasking and Conscious Parenting are like oil and water—they don't mix. Be tuned in and present with your children.

For the best results, try "This one thing," not "These five things."

Let's remember that the simplest activity can become a meditation if we put enough conscious awareness into it.

24. "Thank you for starting your homework," "Thank you for cleaning your room without arguing," or "Thank you for playing so nicely with your brother right now."

Routinely telling our child, "Thank You!" helps make sure we never take our child's positive behavior for granted—plus, it helps ensure a spirit of cooperation forms and settles in.

25. To have a healthy family, a parent must be "the boss" (or, if you prefer, "the leader"). But Mom and Dad exercise their power and authority with firm and loving kindness—with no attempt to control—unless it's a very young child, refusing to take a bath or refusing to stay in their car seat. Then a young child's "I don't have to!" is met with a parent's gentle firmness—"Yes, dear. Yes, you do."

If a parent abdicates this important responsibility, a power vacuum is created. Then a strong-willed child may step in and try to fill that void, becoming, to some degree, demanding, bossy, selfish, and insensitive.

26. If your interactions with your child feel like a tug-of-war, drop the rope. If your interactions with your child feel like you're hitting your head against a wall, go around the wall and figure out a way everyone can work together.

Always try to foster "the team approach."

27. Have a rousing good time with your kids! If you play with them now, they'll be more likely to work with you later.

28. Conscious Parenting is connecting with a child, sharing love, and building bridges.

At the same time, Conscious Parenting is detaching from a child's misbehavior or emotional drama to ensure that love is conveyed and not lost.

29. Parents—make it more about a child's hard work and persistence and less about achievement. Make it more about what a child has learned and less about their grades.

A liberal arts education is available to all. There are no inconvenient classes or super high tuition. All we have to do is open a book, download an audiobook, or just Google something of interest.

Why not try this? At dinner, go around the table and give everyone a chance to describe something they learned that day. After dinner, take turns allowing a family member to look up something interesting on the internet and share it. Or, everyone might want to watch an educational program. Make your home a culture of learning.

 *Education, at its best, can become a continuing adventure in human understanding, shared by all."*

— ADAPTED FROM A QUOTE BY HARRY S. TRUMAN

30. Join your child in "pure learning." This is when a child learns something, but there is no grade attached. Help a child discover subjects they can be passionate about and realize how learning can be its own reward.

This one thing can make conventional school more tolerable as a child realizes that school, however imperfect, is for learning, not just for making good grades.

31.

 *Without a strong educational system, democracy becomes crippled."*

— ADAPTED FROM A QUOTE BY HARRY S. TRUMAN

 *Question everything."*

— SOCRATES

Let's not depend on schools to educate our children. And, let's make sure we teach our kids to think critically and for themselves. If we teach our children to question things (even what we tell them), they will not be so blindly conditioned by society.

1. When a child thinks, "Mom is happy with my behavior," they feel satisfaction. When a child thinks, "Mom is unhappy with my behavior, but she still loves me," they know peace.

2. When we reactively punish a child for their misbehavior, a child can begin to see a parent as insensitive and out of touch. In a word, *mean*. As one can imagine, this does not help and is likely to strain the parent-child relationship.

Instead, let's do our homework. Let's try to figure out what is driving a child's misbehavior. With more understanding, we can more compassionately respond.

 *To understand all is to forgive all."*

— ADAPTED FROM A QUOTE ATTRIBUTED TO
THE BUDDHA

Why not try this? When things are heated, look intently at your child and try to clear your mind. Gaze at them until all the mental labels you have for them begin to fall away (ungrateful, spoiled, selfish, etc.) Now, imagine that you are sending your child "silent love." Imagine love emanating from you and enveloping your child. At this point, whatever you want to say or do will probably be fine. The love is back!

3. Sometimes, we get overly frustrated and upset because we haven't wholly accepted the truth that other people have viewpoints and opinions that are contrary to our own. In other words, we become surprised, over and over again, when we meet a person who doesn't think like we do. But when we accept this important truth, we are free to acknowledge and even appreciate other people's viewpoints and opinions without defensiveness and without a strong emotional reaction.

4. The #1 best way to be a better parent is to talk less and listen more. Tuning in and truly listening says, "I love you," without saying anything at all.

Listening also says, "I care," "I want to understand you," "What you think is important to me," and so much more…

5. Conscious moms and dads never gang up on their kids with criticism or scolding. Instead, they gang up on their kids with positivity and encouragement.

Why not try this? When your child is within earshot, pick up the phone and call Grandma Susan, Uncle Bob, or a family friend. Brag to them about one of your child's recent successes, positive behavior choices, improved behavior score at school, or a time when they were helpful around the house.

(Note: This is not a trick. This is a technique to help a child further strengthen a positive behavior pattern.)

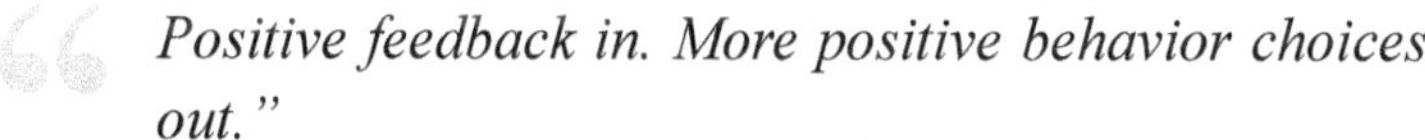

> *Positive feedback in. More positive behavior choices out."*

> — JAY MORGAN

6. Children can make you so happy—and so crazy, sometimes in the same day—or hour, for that matter. Anticipate good behavior, but don't be surprised when the not-so-good behavior comes. Pause. Step back. Be patient, and let strong feelings pass. Deliberate. Then act.

7.

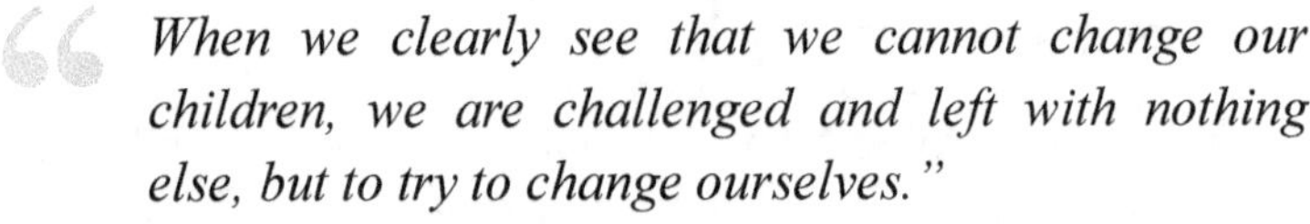

> *When we clearly see that we cannot change our children, we are challenged and left with nothing else, but to try to change ourselves."*

— ADAPTED FROM A QUOTE BY VIKTOR FRANKL

> *When we act more consciously, it is an invitation to our children (and partner) to act more consciously, too."*

— JAY MORGAN

8. The world can be a stressful and sometimes cruel place. Home needs to be a sanctuary; peaceful, so children can get their batteries recharged, and be rejuvenated. How a child views their home life is often how they will come to view the world as they grow up.

> *We need to help insulate our kids, not isolate them."*

— PASTOR FRED LUTER

9. Practice your listening skills. As you listen better, your child will talk more. As they talk more, you will better understand them. As you better understand them, you will naturally be able to parent them better.

10.

> *Most people do not listen with the intent to understand; they listen with the intent to reply."*

— STEPHEN R. COVEY

Psych 101: I admit it. I'm a recovering "feelings scruncher." I used to spend a lot of time and energy scrunching my feelings. Then, I finally figured out what I was doing and, over time, was able to make the necessary adjustments and stop.

Now, I know "feeling scrunching" isn't a very technical term, but it is very descriptive—and remember, I work with children. When I was growing up, feelings were a mystery to me, especially the uncomfortable ones (at the time, I would have called them the "bad feelings"), so I scrunched them. Nobody wants to feel anxious, sad, or angry, so when I had those feelings, I pretended like I didn't. Or, if I couldn't do that much pretending (denial, mixed with a good bit of self-deception), I would tell myself not to feel them. This is when the scrunching began.

As a reflex to the pain I was experiencing, I constricted my feelings. Then I didn't have to feel those unpleasant emotions as much. At first, this was very satisfying. There was less anger, less sadness, and less nervousness. But, little did I know I was only constricting my *conscious awareness of those feelings.* I was still having them; they were just more quickly being redirected to my subconscious mind.

I also discovered I was not only constricting my uncomfortable feelings but my *comfortable feelings as well.* If you crimp a garden hose, the water stops flowing. While I wasn't bothered as much by what I perceived as painful emotions, I wasn't having a lot of nice, pleasant ones either. For a long time, I settled into (and settled for) this very limited feeling state that consisted of varying shades of gray. I had scrunched most of the colorful feelings right out of my life.

In short, I had become a closed system. Feelings were coming in, being quickly denied or suppressed (scrunched), and then they were redirected into my unconscious mind. Nothing was being acknowledged or expressed. My unconscious mind was turning into an emotional swampland.

I finally developed enough insight and self-knowledge to do a major overhaul of my feelings system. I discovered it needed a lot of lubrication and rust remover after all those years of misuse and scrunching. But with a little time, patience, and persistence, I was able to get everything working smoothly again. My feelings center was again *open* for business. From my book *Fingerpainting in Psych Class,* the chapter "Feelings Scruncher."

11. Note to self:

- *Sensitive kids don't hold up very well under a lot of negativity.*
- *All kids are sensitive.*
- *Handle—and parent—with care.*

12. The simple truth is we can't make a child behave just like we can't make a child misbehave. So, let's focus on what we can do. Let's communicate better; let's build a spirit of cooperation; let's praise naturally occurring positive behavior; and let's sparingly implement strategic consequences, but only when positive interventions have failed.

13. Stop rushing. You can't rush Conscious Parenting. Take as much time as you need to engage in a conscious action… so you can keep from engaging in an unconscious reaction.

14. "Silence is golden…" and a pretty good way to go when we don't know what to say or do. In a tense situation—wait. Be patient. There is usually no hurry. And if there is a hurry, we will act—not from thought, but from our instincts.

Psych 101: There are two types of instincts, primary and secondary.

Primary instincts are innate. They are the ones that catapult us out of the way of a speeding car or help us catch a child as they are falling.

Secondary instincts are quite different. They come to us from our egoic mind, but they can also come to us from our higher self.

Egoic instincts can be okay, even good. Others will be all wrong. But instincts from our higher self are inspired. They are often just right for the moment at hand.

15. Arguing is usually one ego bouncing off another—one ego trying to better or dominate another ego. Or, sometimes, the ego feels a powerful need to defend itself. But, once you see it, you begin to rise above it and loosen the ego's influence.

16. The quickest and best way to end an argument is to refuse to participate.

The challenge is to notice when a discussion is turning into an argument and take time away.

Then, schedule a time to continue the discussion when everyone is calm again. Consider making this a mutual agreement with all family members.

17. Seven words that every conscious parent needs to remember: "I'm. Not. Going. To. Argue. With. You." And it's perfectly okay to repeat these words as often as needed.

18. Do you really think a smart, strong-willed child—a child who sometimes wants to do what they want to do a heck of a lot more than they want to do what you want them to do—do you really think that child is *not* going to test you? Really?

19. Regret and guilt suck. Conscious Parenting is much better.

20. Do you have an edgy teen? Irritable? Reactive? Handle them— and yourself—with care. Be pleasant and gracious. Don't take their comments personally. They are suffering from the multi-symptom, serious—but never fatal malady called "Adolescence."

Be the one to smooth the edge off of their edginess.

Case Study: Five-year-old Carson plopped down in his car seat and slammed the door. Something was obviously bothering him. When Mom asked about his day, Carson looked down and said he had only earned two stars that day (four stars were possible). He appeared to be both sad and frustrated by this fact. When Mom asked what happened, Carson said that the teacher "never watched me when I was being good."

Funny, right? But it's also true. We see our kids' behavior problems with 20/20 vision, but so many times miss when they are "being good" or "doing better."

Since this tendency is ingrained, it will likely continue until we train our minds to notice the "good behavior," the "better behavior," or even "the not-so-bad behavior." Welcome to the wonderful world of Conscious Parenting!

21. Kids don't do well with ultimatums. Who does? An ultimatum usually results in a power struggle. After an ultimatum, many kids will think and sometimes angrily say, "You can't make me!" And they're right. Controlling kids is always an illusion.

22. Helping kids works best when help is offered, not pressed upon; when we acknowledge that a child can accept our help or they can reject it.

When a child feels no pressure (no effort to control), they are going to be more open and more likely to accept the help that is being offered.

23.

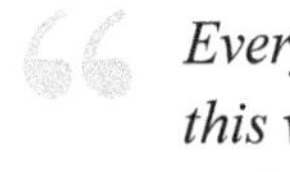

> *Everyone talks about peace, but few teach peace. In this world, competition—being better than another—is forced upon us. We are educated for competition, but some form of competition is the beginning of every war.*
>
> *But when we help a child learn cooperation, and how to affirm others and offer support, that is when we will be educating children for peace."*

— ADAPTED FROM A QUOTE BY MARIA
MONTESSORI

24. Power seeks to control. Love seeks to benevolently influence.

> *When the power of love becomes stronger than the love for power, the world will know peace."*

— JIMI HENDRIX

25. When we are harsh—when we yell or talk down to a child—the child will likely see us as a powerful authority figure… just not a credible and approachable one.

26.

> *"The single greatest talent a therapist can possess is the capacity to be simultaneously both involved and detached. It is not, however, a talent to be developed just by a therapist; It is a capacity that must be developed by anyone who desires to be a healing presence in the world."*

— SCOTT PECK

Buddhists refer to this as the ability to "cry with one eye." What a great way to describe compassion! Being both involved and detached allows our interactions to be nurturing and healing. At the same time, we don't absorb and get caught up in the emotional pain of another. (Note: Our egos are what become attached. But the higher self remains above egoic influence.)

27. While we're doing the work to consciously raise our children, our children transform us. The entire process strips away what is no longer necessary and pushes us to grow in all the many ways available to us.

Why not try this? Start a list of all of the ways that we can grow and discuss them with your child. Here are some: 1) Physically, 2) Mentally, 3) Emotionally, 4) Relationally, 5) Creatively, and 6) Spiritually. Then, name activities and put them in the right group.

Example: Put "Eat a salad" and "Ride my bike" under Physical. Put "Do my homework" and "Do a word puzzle" under Mental, and so on. "Working a puzzle with a sibling" might go under two categories—Mental and Relational.

28. Some parents want to rush the parenting process. They want their child to stop lying, stop aggravating their sister, and stop leaving their bicycle in the driveway. Parents want their children to start doing their homework, start feeding the dog, and start following directions.

But rushing the parenting process is like trying to get a cake to bake faster—if you turn up the heat, you'll burn it. Parenting is an art. You consciously take advantage of opportunities as they present. You just can't force it and do any real good.

29. Many teenagers reactively see work or chores as something to be avoided. If this is the case, you might try saying something like: "Hey, Ellen. It's easy to look at folding clothes, helping your little brother, or cleaning the kitchen as bad. But from a different perspective, you can see them as special ways to help family members—to make things a little easier for everyone. And when you consider this viewpoint, something inside of you gets tender and sensitive. Then, you might begin to see a request that we make of you as an opportunity to help, serve, and learn a new skill—a skill you will likely value throughout your life."

MARCH

1. Not letting kids help because they are "too young," or because it will "just take even longer," or because "It's easier to do it myself" are almost always missed opportunities for building a spirit of giving and cooperation in the parent-child relationship. Let's remember to let kids help.

To become a helper, kids have to learn to focus on others so they can notice how they might be able to help. When we focus on others, there's a tipping point where our own personal issues dissolve and disappear. This is called an outward mindset. See *The Outward Mindset* by the Arbinger Institute for more.

 *Perfect love casts out (and replaces) fear."*

— 1 JOHN 4:18 (PARAPHRASED)

2. It seems impossible for a young child—who has no notion yet of who they are—to grow up feeling good about themselves if they receive a lot of criticism and negativity. However, it seems likely for a young child—who has no notion yet of who they are—to grow up feeling good about themselves if they receive a lot of encouragement and positivity.

3. *The Conscious Parenting secret weapon:* compliment and express appreciation for even small efforts a child makes. And don't criticize or discourage. When we are trying to build a fire, we certainly don't douse it with water. We slowly feed it with kindling. The same goes for helping children. If we want to help a child build a positive behavior pattern, we don't want to "douse it" with criticism and negativity; we want to "feed it" with encouragement and positivity.

4. Are we more interested in good behavior from our children? Or are we more interested in a good relationship? If our efforts go into maintaining a close and healthy relationship, behavior problems will be few.

5. Sometimes, parents get so worried and upset over a child's negative behavior (or emotional issue) that there is more focus and talk about what's wrong than what's right. This can quickly make a bad situation even worse.

Remember, whatever we put energy into is strengthened. So let's put our energy into naturally occurring positive behavior, and let's "reframe" a negative behavior as an improvement over some time in the past (a "reframe" is describing a child's negative behavior in a positive way or in a way that suggests an improvement over a similar behavior in the past).

Why not try this? Ask your child to talk about their day in some detail. The easiest way is for your child to talk about what happened first, second, third, and so on. At certain points, a parent can say, "Okay. Let me see if I'm following along." Then, they can reflect back to the child what they heard them say. The child can even give the parent a letter grade on how well they're listening and understanding. This is a great exercise to help kids be more open with their thoughts, feelings, and experiences. And to seal the deal, parents should regularly share parts of their day, too.

6. A child's misbehavior can push us into more unconsciousness. Or, with patience and understanding, it will propel us into greater consciousness and personal growth.

7. Children can hurt our feelings and make us angry. But, at these times, if we can extend kindness and love through our words and actions, hard feelings will more likely soften and not build up. This can then initiate the forgiveness process and make it easier to deal with a child patiently and with compassion.

8. If we don't make a conscious plan to stay close to our child (or partner), we will likely begin to drift apart. Conflicted feelings and a lack of forgiveness can sabotage any relationship. A healthy relationship, therefore, has to be consciously developed and consciously maintained.

9. "My child is so stubborn! He fights with me all the time! He'll never amount to anything!" Or, with a more conscious perspective, "My child is so stubborn! It won't be easy, but if we do this right, our child will go far and do great things!" Same child. Different perspective.

Case Study: Fifteen-year-old Debbie was definitely a fighter. She routinely argued with her parents and her teachers. She fought with her friends. Any time her mom or dad wanted her to clean her room, do her homework or watch her little brother, you could bet there was going to be a fight. Sometimes, she would fight so long that she would actually get out of doing things. Her mom would look at her, shake her head, and say, "Never mind, Debbie. I'll just do it myself." So sometimes, there were payoffs to her fighting.

For the most part, Debbie stayed in trouble. She was constantly grounded—and it was constantly "not her fault." It was her parents' fault, her teacher's fault, her little brother's fault, or anybody else's fault. Debbie was always the victim.

So Debbie and I started meeting. She was a frustrating case. With Debbie, arguing seemed to be an art form. She was truly a master. The more I discussed things with her, the more steadfast she defended her position. I hung in there but quickly realized I was out of my league. She was wearing me out. I needed something different to reach beyond her extremely well-defended psyche. Then, during one session, it came to me.

As I verbally sparred with her, an old memory popped into my mind. I immediately sensed that sharing this story could help. I paused to collect my thoughts, then said, "Debbie, as I was listening to you just now, a memory came to me. When I was 14 years old, I tried to earn my swimming merit badge at Boy Scout camp. To earn it, I had to swim one mile in the Saline River. The staff had a quarter-mile course marked off with some buoys right out in the middle of the river. The other boys and I took a boat to the first buoy and jumped in.

"I casually swam downstream for a quarter mile. This first leg wasn't bad at all. Then I rounded the buoy and started swimming upstream, against the current, back to where we began. That second leg wasn't easy at all. I had to swim constantly because if I stopped, I would start drifting back downstream.

"I barely made it that second quarter-mile. I rounded the buoy and was thankful I was again swimming with the current. As I swam, I was able to catch my breath because the current carried me along.

"When I rounded the last buoy and started swimming upstream again, I thought I just might make it. I swam hard, trying to go against the current, but I quickly used up my last bit of energy. I called for the boat that was following the swimmers to pick me up. Needless to say, I didn't get my swimming merit badge that day."

Debbie was attentive during my story. She never once interrupted. I smiled at her and continued.

"Now, you're probably wondering why we're talking about me and my swimming merit badge. Well, let me explain. We've spent a good bit of time getting to know each other, and sometimes, you remind me of a person swimming upstream. You often seem to be swimming against the current. Everything is such a struggle with you.

"It seems to me that your life, my life, everybody's life has a flow to it. When a person goes with the flow of life, things are typically easier. They don't get tired so quickly. They use the current to move themselves along. But there are many times you seem to go against that natural flow of life. You fight against people and situations when the best thing to do would be to go with the flow. Doesn't that sometimes just make you tired? Have you ever thought about relaxing and going with the current? Have you ever just felt like letting the current carry you along for a while?"

Debbie was uncharacteristically quiet. She looked at me for a moment. I couldn't tell by her expression what she thought of my anecdote, so we went on to discuss one or two goals for the upcoming week, and then our time was up.

During the next several meetings, Debbie's parents reported she was less argumentative. She was, at times, even cooperative. Daily life at home wasn't such a struggle. Her parents were good about complimenting Debbie on being more of a team player.

In one session, shortly before we terminated, Debbie surprised me. We were talking about school and friends, and when there was a pause, she looked at me and said, "I wanted to tell you that I liked your story. I think it helped me see things differently. It was a good story."

Debbie then shared with me how she was now making some decisions that seemed to go with the current of life, not against it. She told me that, in many situations, it was indeed easier and more satisfying to go with the flow of things.

I told Debbie I was happy my story had helped. I complimented her for being able to swim with the current when it was in her best interest to do so. I let her know there would be times in her life when she would again need to go against the current, as with her decisions involving peer pressure. And, I reminded her, at those times, the practice she had of swimming against the current would come in very handy. I was confident Debbie would continue to improve her ability to maneuver through the currents of life.

From *Fingerpainting in Psych Class*, the chapter "Swimming Upstream."

10. Sometimes, kids close down. They pull away from a parent and stop confiding in them. I teach children that feelings have a small weight to them. Ignoring their feelings and never sharing them will cause feelings to "stack up" and accumulate. Then feelings build up on the inside and begin to weigh a child down. This is when emotional problems can occur—exaggerated expressions of anger, sadness, or fear. And these accumulated feelings can even affect a child's attitude and behavior. Talking openly is usually the first way kids learn to release their feelings and keep things "light" on the inside.

Why not try this? Ask your child to lift and hold a chair. See how long they can hold it before it gets too heavy, and they want to put it down. This is a great illustration of how it feels when we hold everything in and keep everything to ourselves.

Next, the adult holds one side of the chair while the child holds the other. In this exercise, a child can easily see that sharing the weight of the chair is a much better way to go. It is the very same with our personal lives and experiences—sharing thoughts and feelings with a special someone is much better than trying to keep everything to ourselves.

11. Feelings that are not expressed come out through a child's behavior. This is one of the reasons why feelings identification and expression exercises are so important. A child can't talk about a feeling until they can name it.

Why not try this? Make up a story with your child. The adult begins. To illustrate, let's say the story is about a porcupine named

Larry and his new friend, Lucas, a floppy-eared rabbit. Larry and Lucas are playing frisbee. They are having great fun! Then they both reach down to pick up the frisbee at the same time, and Larry accidentally pokes Lucas with several of his quills! You end your part of the story by saying, "And this made Lucas feel______?"

Then, the story is passed on to your child. They try to name how Lucas might feel after getting stuck by the quills (Note: You might want to download a copy of different feelings to use as a guide or, better yet, make your own). A parent can also ask how Larry probably felt being the one responsible for sticking Lucas, even though it was an accident.

Now it's your child's turn. They make up their part of the story and again stop at the point where the character is experiencing another emotion. Now, it's the parent's turn to guess how the character probably feels in this new situation. Continue the story and take turns naming the different feelings. Always try to end the story on a high note. If one storyline bogs down, try another.

Added Bonus: This exercise utilizes imagination and creativity to help a child playfully learn about and understand feelings.

12. Some kids are born with a strong-willed temperament. They have to learn to use their strong will to do what their parents want them to do, not what they may selfishly want to do. To the degree a child is successful, they free themselves of unhealthy selfishness, and their strong will becomes one of their greatest assets. To the degree they are unsuccessful, unhealthy selfishness settles in, and their strong will can become one of their greatest liabilities.

13. When we try to make a child do something, we can needlessly create a power struggle.

"You WILL clean your room! Today!" Sounds strong, right? No nonsense.

The only problem is that it is unenforceable! No parent can MAKE a child clean their room. And kids know that. Strong-willed kids can have a field day when a parent slips into the "illusion of control."

As difficult as it may be, a parent must consciously *honor* a child's free will to follow directions and, yes, to *not* follow directions. Let your focus be on building a spirit of cooperation between you and your child, noticing instances where they are listening, and being a little more cooperative than some time in the past.

> *There's a world of difference between insisting that a child do something, and creating an atmosphere in which a child can grow into wanting to do it."*
>
> — ADAPTED FROM A QUOTE BY MISTER ROGERS

Psych 101: When something or someone activates a "trigger" (an old, unconscious reaction fueled by the fight-or-flight reflex), there is a physiological response you can actually feel in your body. At that moment, go into your body and notice what's happening. Choose to feel the sensations—heat, cold, tightness, clinching, or shaking. Whatever is happening, be there as the silent observer. Just watch.

Now, use the muscles involved to exaggerate your physical reaction. Tighten any muscles being clenched, hold, and then release them. If you're shaking, shake more vigorously and for a longer time. Imagine that you're shaking out or squeezing toxins from your body.

This exercise can help weaken deep, long-standing, conditioned physiological reactions and make way for healing and wholeness.

14. Sure, it would be easier if your child would just be quiet and do what you say… But then you wouldn't have a child—you'd have a robot.

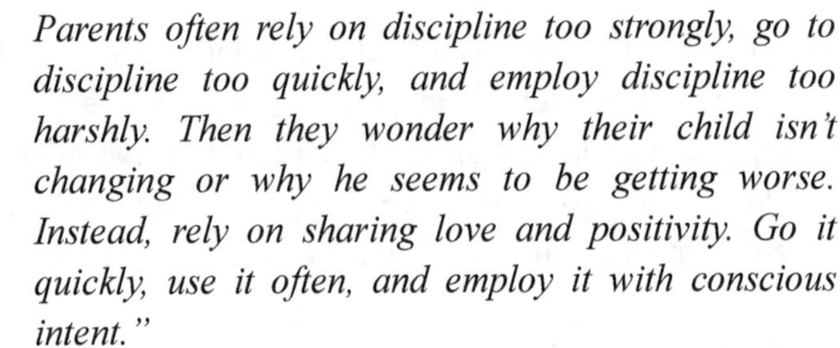

> *Parents often rely on discipline too strongly, go to discipline too quickly, and employ discipline too harshly. Then they wonder why their child isn't changing or why he seems to be getting worse. Instead, rely on sharing love and positivity. Go it quickly, use it often, and employ it with conscious intent."*

— JAY MORGAN

15.

> *Your child is not attention seeking. Your child is attachment seeking."*

— DR. VANESSA LAPOINTE

Not all attachments are created equal. Kids will sometimes try to establish a negative attachment through their misbehavior or by exaggerating their emotions. At these times, parents must try not to react negatively but draw them back to positive behavior by conveying love, by using strategic positive cuing, and by using a reframe (A reframe is describing a child's negative behavior in a positive way or in a way that suggests an improvement over a similar behavior from the past).

16. Maybe parents try too hard to make a child feel important (have high self-esteem) instead of helping them understand, discover, and experience their innate importance. Discovering this kind of importance can only come through spiritual (or metaphysical) understanding and practice. (i.e., meditation, yoga, inner bodywork, spiritual teachings, etc.) See *The Little Book of Sutras* for more on this topic.

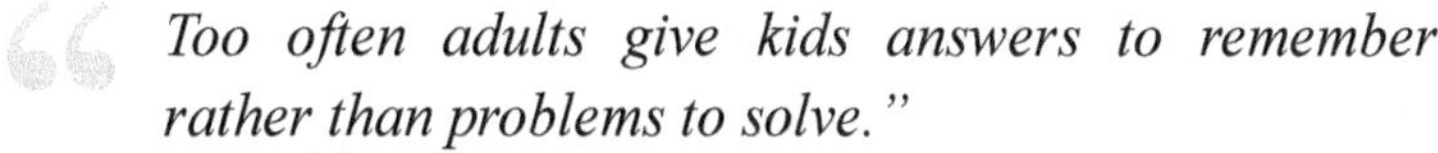

> *The unfettered soul of a free man offers a spiritual defense unconquered and unconquerable."*
>
> — HARRY S. TRUMAN

17.

> *Too often adults give kids answers to remember rather than problems to solve."*
>
> — ROGER LEWIN

Conscious Parenting helps us learn how to share information so a child can see the answer for themself—no spoon-feeding required.

18. The healthiest relationships contain spaciousness so each person has room to grow; they have love so emotional closeness is maintained, and there is mutual respect so each person feels free to be themself.

19. Don't be stingy with your "Thank you's." Tell your child, 'Thank you for listening,' 'Thank you for following directions the first time,' 'Thank you for giving good eye contact,' and 'Thank you for being patient.' Saying 'thank you' is one of the simplest ways to build cooperation in the parent-child relationship and to keep things going right.

20. Children need to consistently receive the message, "I like you just the way you are." Then, a child will feel secure in the parent-child relationship and come closer to discovering their authentic self—and not grow into the self they think their parents want them to be.

21. Engaging in activities that raise our conscious awareness puts more consciousness in us so that we can put more consciousness in our child.

22.

> *When you create a problem, you create pain. All it takes is a simple choice, a simple decision: No matter what happens, I will create no more pain for myself. I will create no more problems."*

— ECKHART TOLLE

Most pain comes from thinking about our past or anxiously anticipating some future event. When we practice present-moment awareness, all of that breaks down and our sanity returns.

> *It's funny. The mind is the only place where we can create a problem before we have an actual problem."*

— JAY MORGAN

Why not try this? Being more in touch with our physical sensations can help us be more in touch with our emotional feelings.

Sit down with your child and take turns tuning into one of the five senses—touch, hearing, seeing, smelling, and tasting. Ask your child, "What do you feel right now? or "What do you hear right now?" and so on. Provide them with some interesting things to taste and smell to turn on those senses. Take your time and let them really get into it.

Being in touch with our five senses immediately puts us in the now moment, slows our thinking, and helps us to be more fully centered in our body. And we must be in our bodies to start to pick up on our emotional feelings.

23. It would be nice if parenting was like cooking a microwave dinner. You talk with your child for 90 seconds, and it's done. Your child is changed!

But Conscious Parenting is hardly ever like that. It's more like ultra-slow, low-heat cooking. Get ready to take your time. Observe your child. Deliberate. Then, you can take full advantage of each opportunity as it arises.

24. A little time alone makes the time with the little ones a little easier.

25. As parents, we must train ourselves to notice our children's "naturally occurring positive behaviors" and make a big deal out of them.

My word picture for this is a young child learning to stand up. I remember my daughter pulling up on a table and trying to get her feet underneath her. Everyone in the room would stop what they were doing, smile, and cheer: "Hooray! Hannah's standing up!" Hannah would literally beam.

We want to provide a lot of positive energy, even for small things. This draws children away from any secondary gain they may get from their negative behavior. (Secondary gain is when a child allows themself to feel good about something that is inherently negative or unhealthy.)

At the same time, we must learn to respond to negative behaviors —problem behaviors—with little to no energy. And we want to use as few words as possible. A parent might even want to rehearse or come up with a generic phrase so that not too much emotion goes into it. ("You know it's not okay to push your sister. Go sit on your bed and think about what you did and how it made your sister feel. Then we can talk in a little while.")

26. "Wu Wei" is a Taoist term that means one's actions spring forth effortlessly from the natural flow of life. With Wu Wei, decisions are arrived at (or, more accurately, come to us) through stillness and silence. There is no strain or deliberation. And these decisions are only there when we need them—a perfect response to the situation at hand.

27.

> *Behind every child who believes in themself is a parent who believed in them first."*
>
> — ADAPTED FROM A QUOTE BY MATTHEW L. JACOBSON

28. Many parents reactively tell their children what they like about their behavior and what they don't like about their behavior.

On the surface, this may sound okay. But many times, this can push a child into trying to be the child they think their parents want them to be. This process is very subtle and can happen even with the best intentions.

Then children find themselves trapped on an imaginary treadmill of trying to please their parents—doing the things their parents like while trying not to do the things their parents don't like.

Kids then try to grow into their parents' projection of them and, in the process, cave to parental pressure. These now unacceptable parts of themselves (physical parts or certain aspects of their personality) are lost, suppressed into the psyche, or, as Carl Jung called it, "the shadow part of ourselves."

Sometimes, defiance and rebellion can be a strong-willed child's attempt to maintain their autonomy and their developing sense of self. Not cooperating with parents, especially the over-controlling ones, literally becomes a desperate attempt to save what the child considers to be their genuine self. In this situation, many impulses to be uncooperative and defiant actually arise from the healthy part of a child's personality, not the unhealthy part.

29. When a parent nags, scolds, and lectures, it irritates children. It also says, "You need me to be over-involved, supervise you constantly, and spell things out for you."

When a parent takes the time to simply say what needs to be said, a child is more likely to listen. We try to relate the message: "You're smart. You know what I am talking about. You've got this."

30. Let's affirm our child's thoughts and feelings. We shouldn't automatically challenge or discount them or try to convince our children they're wrong to think or feel a certain way.

Remember, we are talking about a unique, one-of-a-kind little person—not an extension of ourselves. Instead, let's focus on fully understanding our child, fully understanding where our child is coming from, what they think, and what they believe.

31. When a parent is critical, over time, some children simply cannot keep going. They become discouraged, procrastinate or give up. This is their unconscious reaction to an overly critical parent. The child's newly developing psyche can simply not stand up to that much criticism. What a tragedy! Let's go positive instead.

APRIL

1. As long as a parent thinks their child must talk to them more respectfully than they talk to their child, all is lost.

2. When a parent tries to impose their will on a child, they see their child more as an extension of themselves, not as a smaller human being with free will. Children have free will to listen and cooperate, and they have free will to NOT listen and NOT cooperate. Don't attempt the impossible! Instead, focus on connection, positivity, relating felt love, and building a spirit of cooperation.

Psych 101: Let's imagine that you and your teenager are visiting the Grand Canyon. In this hypothetical situation, you are tied to a tree while your teenager is wearing a blindfold, walking around— shaky, and disoriented. What can you do? What is there to help keep your teenager from blindly walking off the side of the cliff? You can't reach out and grab them.

If you think about it, all we have is trust and the bond we have established with our teen. This bond is formed by consistently conveying love and through conscious communication. Let's try to work on these things daily. Then, if our child is in a bad place, they will be more likely to come to us for help.

3. Your psychological state, attitude, and behavior say, "I'm open and available," or it says, "I'm busy and preoccupied." Be open, and available.

4. When a parent harshly reacts to a child's belligerence or misbehavior, the child will automatically project and focus on the inappropriateness of the parent's behavior… and no longer focus on the inappropriateness of their own.

5. When a parent's approach becomes harsh and negative, a child closes down to what they perceive as a threat. Then, they will no longer take in, and benefit from positive and potentially helpful information a parent tries to share. In short, they become a closed system—either afraid or angry and resentful. Instead, let's spend our energy to keep things going right.

6. Unconsciously scolding a child might make them feel inadequate and inferior. And what parent would consciously want to make their child feel inadequate and inferior?

Why not try this? Today, see if you can elicit a child's cooperation on several tasks. Work together. Then identify three times when you can say, "Thanks for working with me on that!" or "You're getting to be such a great helper!"

7. Be sure to comment on a child's behavior when it is good. And make sure to convey love when it isn't.

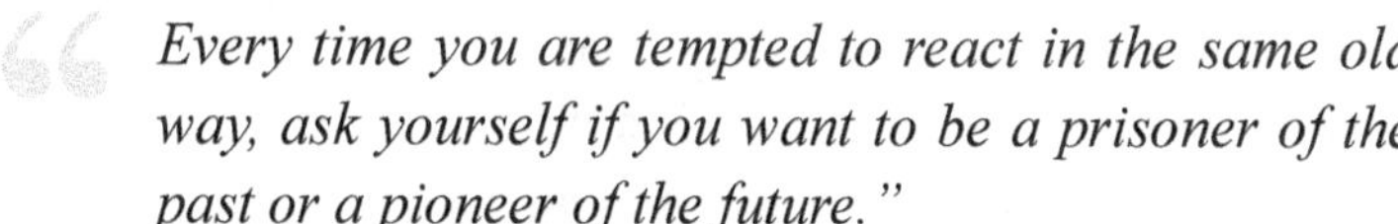

> *Every time you are tempted to react in the same old way, ask yourself if you want to be a prisoner of the past or a pioneer of the future."*

— DEEPAK CHOPRA

Conscious parents break away from old, reactive behavior patterns, so we are pioneers of the future, working to build healthier and more conscious families.

8. You find calmness in yourself, not in the middle of a domestic drama. If you lose your centeredness, you're probably getting pulled into the drama. Go to your breathing and allow it to be your anchor.

9. Love that is not felt means little. Love that is related inconsistently—or marred by anger and harshness—might make a child question where they stand in the parent-child relationship.

Case Study: Do you have a teen who is drifting into some negative activities?

"John, when you were little, I would often hold your hand, particularly when we were crossing the street or a parking lot. I held your hand to keep you safe and because I love you. Sometimes you wanted to go your own way—to dart off into danger—so I would have to tighten my grip and pull you closer.

"Now you're a teenager. I don't hold your hand anymore. That would be silly. You're way too old and mature for that. But this process of loving you and trying to keep you safe is still active. When you 'dart off into danger'—when you do things that aren't right for you—my reaction is to tighten my grip and pull you closer. This is why I have to restrict your activities when you do things I believe will hurt you and jeopardize your future. This is my way of trying to keep you safe, and it's still because I love you —not because I want to give you a hard time.

"Please, John, settle down a little. Walk with me a while longer... Don't be so eager to dart off in any direction that looks interesting. I don't want to scare you—Life is wonderful. I just want to protect you a little longer until you're ready to deal with all the subtleties of life—things that might lure you into something that feels good at first, but then derails your life and leaves you feeling empty."

Kids feel good about healthy things, but kids can drift where they allow themselves to feel good about unhealthy things, too. A young person can feel good about making the honor roll, they can feel good about making the dance team, or they can feel good about adding to their baseball card collection. But, kids can also feel good about getting out of doing their homework, stealing something from Target, or throwing a fit so they get out of having to clean their room. They can allow themselves to feel good about these behaviors, too.

Feeling good about a healthy activity is natural. It just happens. But feeling good about an unhealthy activity is always an acquired taste. Plus, there are always hidden price tags. Feeling good about unhealthy things greatly complicates a child's life and starts developing into what I call "negative self-esteem." And then, as the saying goes, once you create a monster, you have to feed it. Kids can get stuck and venture deeper into these negative, unhealthy, self-defeating behaviors. And tragically, some never find their way out. See *Fingerpainting In Psych Class* for more.

10. A parent's self-restraint involves amazing inner strength—which will often be mistaken for weakness by the casual observer.

11. Every time we love, connect, and empathize with our child, their brain and body get flooded with feel-good hormones. Imagine this building and strengthening millions of neural pathways in your child's brain—soothing them, and making it easier for them to regulate their emotions, empathize, create, and make well-thought-out decisions.

12. The love we have for our children is the best motivator, pushing us to parent them better and more consciously.

13. Generally, the more positive we are, the less negative our kids' behavior will be. Remember the adage: "Give what you want to get."

The exception is when parents try to be positive with kids, but their old negativity is still there—and it's just enough to keep a child's negative behavior in place.

Parents have to trust that positivity will work, even if they don't see immediate results.

14. Many people like to go window shopping. This is when we leisurely walk around the mall, making off-the-cuff comments: "Oh, look at those shoes! They are so cool!" Or, "Look at that dress! It's hideous!"

If we are not careful, "window shopping parenting" will creep into our relationship with our children. This is when a parent tells a child what they like about their behavior, but then, with just as much enthusiasm, they tell their kids what they don't like about their behavior. Window-shopping parenting can put kids on the imaginary treadmill of trying to please their parents, or it can fill them with anger and resentment.

15. Today—right now—this moment. This is the only time you will have with your kids. Make it count!

Why not try this? "Stewart was really pushing my buttons this morning!"

Don't blame your child for pushing your buttons—thank them. Then they are easier to locate and disconnect. In psychology, this process is called desensitization.

16. Positive comments generate positive feelings in our children, while negative comments generate negative feelings. It's just about that simple.

And one of the most positive feelings we can generate in our children is the feeling of love.

When we create the intention (or plan) to love, what we say and do will be filled with and enveloped in our love. This becomes our gift—a gift that will be received and embraced by our children. This is one important way we take our felt love and instill that love into our kids.

17. To a child, overcorrection and reactive criticism are like poking them with a sharp stick. Ouch!

Noticing a child's positive behavior (along with noticing the *absence of negative behavior*) is a much better way to go.

"You cleaned your room with less of a negative attitude. I bet that felt better than cleaning your room in an angry way like last week."

"We've all been up for a couple of hours. We had breakfast, and we went on a walk. In all that time, no one has aggravated or gotten into an argument. I could get used to this!"

18. We soothe an angry or upset child with our own inner calmness. Our inner calmness must come first, before we say or do anything. If we start to talk or act when we are upset, our words and actions can easily upset things further.

19. Raising kids can evoke fear.

Parents think, "What if my child keeps doing this? Or, "What if my child never learns to do that? What will become of them?!?!?

Fear is understandable but ultimately becomes a psychological barrier to Conscious Parenting. If a parent is afraid, fear will be expressed, consciously and unconsciously, through their words and actions. Then we will have a child who is not all that confident they can change or reach some desired goal. And they may start to believe that their parents aren't that confident in them either…

20. No one will have more influence on your child than you.

Why not try this? If children only do the right thing because they are afraid to do the wrong thing—they are afraid to get in trouble, be consequenced or punished—they have not internalized the desired behavior.

Kids need help realizing that positive and adaptive behaviors "feel better" (they are a better fit) and help create a higher quality of life. In essence, engaging in positive behavior creates its own reward.

When a child experiences this truth, the problem behaviors will no longer be a problem.

21. Parents must generate faith and verbalize belief in a child, pointing out past successes or times when a child worked hard, did not give up, and persevered. Parents relate confidence that a child has learned a lesson, can change a behavior pattern, or can reach a desired goal. In short, parents must be their child's confidence, until they are able to develop their own.

22. Are you interested in what's right for your child? Or are you more interested in what YOU think is right for your child?

Being interested in what's right for your child is being "child-focused," which will likely lead to a satisfactory course of action. Being interested in what YOU think is right for your child is "parent-focused." This is seeing your child through the screen of your own mental expectations and is likely to lead to a course of action that is unsatisfactory because a child's viewpoint is not consciously considered.

A parent's message is then, "You need to become what I think you should become. I know better than you who you are and how best to live your life."

Why not try this? Look intently at your child with "silent love." Take a moment to remind yourself of how much you love them. Allow your feelings of love to move to the forefront of your awareness. When we remind ourselves of the true feelings we have for our children, unconscious reactions will not be possible.

23. We can't just learn coping skills to manage anxiety and stress. This will always be a short-term solution. If we rely on coping skills, anxiety and stress will eventually overcome us, again and again. The only long-lasting and permanent fix for managing anxiety and stress is to become a calmer person…

24. When it comes to helping a child feel loved, one minute of undivided attention is better than one hour of scattered attention.

Why not try this? Many times when we're playing with a child, we have to go do something else. If this becomes a pattern, a child might feel slighted. Now and then, when you have time, be with a child until *they* are ready to do something else. This sends a beautiful message to your child and keeps them from thinking you've got better things to do than hang out with them.

25. Self-compassion is better than self-love.

Self-compassion is loving ourselves but also being patient and understanding with ourselves—with our weaknesses and blind spots. It's forgiving ourselves each and every time we fall short. Self-compassion helps us learn something new, something better. It allows us to push forward in a gentle way and never give up.

Psych 101: When I was in my 40s, I sat down to talk with my dad. When the moment was right, I asked Dad why he so rarely gave us praise when we were children. To my recollection, I don't remember my dad ever saying, "I'm proud of you," something every kid would be delighted to hear.

Dad didn't even pause. He said he didn't compliment us because "Good behavior is its own reward."

I immediately recognized the wisdom in this statement. When we make good behavior choices, we can expect good things to come our way. When we make good choices, we don't have to worry about getting in trouble, and our conscience is clear. And there's something about making a good choice that just feels better than making a bad one.

The only thing my dad didn't seem to understand was that kids don't immediately know this. We have to compliment young children, so they come to realize what behaviors are positive and adaptive, and what behaviors are negative and maladaptive.

26. What parents say to a child, and how they say it, not only "registers," but strongly influences, and directly impacts how a child sees themself. The younger the child, the more our words impact them.

27. When a loved one emotionally hurts us, resisting the reactive impulse to hurt them back is conscious self-control at its best. Extending grace (unmerited, or unearned favor), kindness, and love at these difficult times is person-changing, situation-changing, and relationship-changing.

28. For many people, critical thinking becomes their way of viewing others.

Critical people usually want to help (or sometimes "straighten someone out"), but they mistakenly believe their criticism will "open another person's eyes" and help them to "see the error of their ways."

In actuality, criticism—especially harsh criticism—only makes another person feel attacked, so they withdraw, defend themselves, or attack back.

The Fix: Stop using unbridled criticism and negativity. Instead, focus on the positive, the good, and the improvement in other people. Try to keep things going right. And don't wait for things to go wrong.

29. Many parents never realize the power of positive parenting because they continue to make reactive, negative statements. They like one behavior, but they strongly dislike another. This dilutes and negates the power of previously made positive comments. A child may then continue to chase after a parent's praise or approval, or they may settle for the devious satisfaction of connecting with a parent through some negative behavior. Then, the parent remains confused and frustrated. And the child never makes the shift to getting their emotional needs met through a parent's loving and affirming positive attention.

30. Adversity in a relationship is unavoidable.

If you deal with it reactively, adversity will, in all likelihood, create hard feelings, pull you and another person apart, and damage the relationship. But, if you address it consciously, adversity can be a catalyst for personal growth. It can help you transcend the ego and guide you to employ strategies that have the potential to pull you and another person closer than ever before.

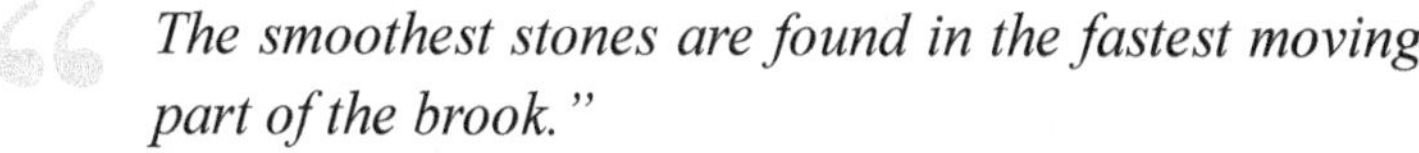

The smoothest stones are found in the fastest moving part of the brook."

— ZEN PROVERB

Friction can smooth things out if we don't allow it to tear things apart."

— JAY MORGAN

1. If something is making you mad hours later, you are mentally revisiting it and keeping it alive in your mind. Divert your attention. Drop it. Come back to the now moment. With no angry thinking, anger evaporates quickly. Then, teach your child how to do this, too.

Why not try this? When children are upset—when they are angry, nervous, or sad—they are trapped in a negative thought loop. Remember, angry thoughts create angry feelings, nervous thoughts create nervous feelings, and sad thoughts create sad feelings.

When children get upset, a parent might try using The Five Questions. Ask your child if they would like to feel better—would they like to feel less angry? Would they like to feel less nervous or less sad? Hopefully, they will want to feel better and agree to try this exercise. But sometimes, a child is consumed by strong emotions, and they might tell you, "No!" and "Leave me alone!" Then, they are obviously not ready for The Five Questions.

But, if a child does want to feel better, ask them five questions. For example, you might ask questions with the "favorites theme"—"What's your favorite dessert?" or "What's your favorite kind of pizza?" or "What's your favorite thing to do in the summer?" and so on.

Children are likely to get an emotional lift or even start smiling when they think about and talk about their favorite things. Then you can ask your child, "Where did the anger go?" Or where did their nervousness or sadness go?

The child then might get pulled right back into their negative thought loop, but you showed them, and they briefly saw, something important: When they started thinking and talking about positive things, they were no longer thinking angrily or nervously, or in a sad way. Those negative thought patterns began to weaken and dissolve.

Note: Kids should never try to block their negative thoughts—Just skip over them. Then, they focus on something positive and pleasant. And children shouldn't feel any pressure from this exercise. They are just using a technique they know will make them feel better.

2. Kind words and actions make for a kind person. Unkind words and unkind actions pollute a person's inner and outer world.

3. Just because we think it and just because we feel it, doesn't mean it needs to be said. Words are more powerful than we can imagine.

4. You can try to change a family member, or you can try to love them more perfectly. An atmosphere of love and acceptance creates the perfect environment for self-exploration and growth.

5. If we are going to be conscious parents, we have to give up the felt need to reactively punish our children when they anger or upset us.

6. Let's speak to children in love—with love behind our words. This actually has a chance of working.

7. Children who were raised by very unconscious parents have more difficulty learning how to be conscious parents to their kids. But often, they are the most motivated to do so.

At first, unconscious parenting is the norm. Then we wake up… We see and hear the automatic-ness of our reactive responses. We see and hear the same old verbal exchanges repeated between family members. We become determined to stop the old and reach out for something new. We begin to pull free. We carefully choose our words. Our actions are more calculated. We become a true force for good.

8. Say what you mean, but don't say it means. Conscious parents try to talk in a way that helps—and not in a way that hurts a child, strains the relationship, or makes a situation worse.

Case Study: Fourteen-year-old Malcolm came into our meeting, obviously feeling good. But in the previous session, he had been very sad and angry. Malcolm had gone on and on, complaining about school, his over-controlling parents, and the track coach who never seemed to give him a break. He told me that, in his opinion, life really wasn't worth living. Now, here he was, just two weeks later, feeling upbeat and light-hearted.

I commented on my observation. "Malcolm, it seems like you feel better today, and I'm glad. Last time, you looked so sad and angry."

Malcolm almost did not let me finish. He reactively continued my line of thought by saying, "...but I shouldn't be in a good mood!" Malcolm then started going through the laundry list of everything that was going wrong for him and everything that he anticipated would go wrong for him in the future.

Now, it was my turn to interrupt. "Malcolm. Whoa. Slow down." I gently said. "Let's go back. You almost admitted that, yes, you were in a good mood. But then, a thought must have jumped in your mind. That thought seemed to forcefully remind you that 'No, you're Malcolm' and 'Malcolm doesn't have good moods.' Then it spouted out all the reasons a good mood is out of the question for you. Where did all of that come from?"

Malcolm listened but didn't answer. I suggested there was something important going on in his mind, something of which he needed to be aware.

"Malcolm, I learned in school that there are these things called conditioned thought patterns," I said. "They are like voice tapes that play in our minds. From what you just said, I am confident that you have one of these tapes. This 'voice' just tried to convince you that you don't deserve to feel happy, even for a moment. The voice tried to convince you that your life is too hard, hopeless, and will never change.

"But Malcolm," I continued. "I have some good news. This tape that tells you that your life is no good only works if you believe what it tells you. If you learn to notice when it starts and remind yourself that it's just an old perspective from your past, it will begin to lose its power over you. And, if you decide to create a new perspective—focusing on things that are going right for you and things you can look forward to in the future—the whole tape will begin to disintegrate like in the "Mission Impossible" movies. Now, let me teach you a simple form of meditation to get you started…"

9. One reason parents get mad so quickly is that we unconsciously presume a child has the same thoughts, feelings, attitudes, and beliefs that we have.

When it becomes obvious that they don't, some parents reactively try to "convert" a child to their viewpoint before they have done the work of fully understanding their child's viewpoint.

10. Just because we see critically—which helps us identify a potential problem—doesn't mean we have to speak critically.

Why not try this? Play the "I Like Game." Sit with your child(ren) for five minutes during lunch or a quiet-seat activity. Notice and comment on all the things you like about them and their behavior choices. Include comments on some behaviors they are not engaging in, like "not arguing" or "not being off task." Playing the I Like Game will quickly help a parent notice all the positive behavior they may have been missing.

11. Words are powerful! Our words and tone can push a child away—hurt, scare, or anger them—or draw them into an adversarial relationship. However, our words and tone can also draw a child into a cooperative relationship characterized by love and mutual respect. For this reason, conscious parents make their communication count, using their words carefully, strategically, and with self-control.

12. Trying to orchestrate outer peace before we achieve a certain amount of inner peace won't work. When we are peaceful, we emanate calm. When we are agitated but try to appear peaceful, it is something, but usually not enough. Either a person will draw us into their agitation, or we will draw them into our peace.

13. When we are so immersed in the now moment… When the past and the future no longer have any significant influence on what we say and do with our child, we have arrived. Welcome to Conscious Parenting!

14. If we want to raise free thinkers and non-conformists—adults who are in a position to "shake things up" and make a positive difference in the world—we have to quit freaking out or becoming enraged when our child disagrees, challenges us, or refuses to blindly conform to our wishes.

Psych 101: If a 3-year-old falls and skins their knee, everyone knows it. They scream. They cry. They want their mama! For young children, this type of reaction is expected and comes as no big surprise.

As children grow up, they are given frequent warnings so they don't get hurt. By the time they start kindergarten, almost every child has heard, "Don't touch that stove! It's hot!" or, "Don't run in the house! You'll fall down! or, "Get away from that outlet! You'll get electrocuted!" Adults teach kids that physical pain is to be avoided. "Be careful," we say, "Try not to get hurt." But then, inevitably, a young child will experience emotional pain with no physical injury.

Four-year-old Lacey was in the nursery at church. When her parents picked her up, she was crying inconsolably. The childcare worker said Lacey and another little girl named Tara disagreed about what to play. Tara had gotten mad and told Lacey, "I'm not going to be your friend anymore!" This was a new kind of hurt for Lacey. She cried for about 15 minutes before she finally calmed down. No blood, no bruises, no broken bones—but plenty of pain.

Initially, young children are wide open with their feelings. They are 100% happy, or 100% sad, or 100% angry, and so on. But then kids change. Slowly, kids begin to "try not to get hurt," as their parents taught them. While kids can avoid many kinds of physical pain by being careful, emotional pain doesn't work that way. For a young child, this kind of pain is unavoidable.

This is the time when kids begin to discover their psychological defense mechanisms. They become, to some degree, closed and dishonest when they are feeling uncomfortable. However, teaching our children to name their feelings and talk about them can minimize the need to be closed and dishonest about how they feel. Many future emotional issues can then be avoided.

Adults are just children, with layers."

— WOODY HARRELSON

15. "I can talk to you any way I want! I'm your parent!" said the unconscious parent. But here's a newsflash: Your child can talk to you any way they want, too. Let's try not to give kids an excuse to be disrespectful.

16. When your strong-willed child is fighting you but eventually complies, a Conscious Parent might say, "You just gave me a very hard time, but then something changed. In your mind, you decided to work with me. That's exciting! Sometimes it's hard for you to cooperate, but it's so important. Thanks for working on that!"

17. Don't think, "Punish them!" Think, "Understand, and help them."

18. You get to decide how you will touch your child's life—today, and every day.

19. When our child is upset and hurting, we reflexively soothe and comfort them. But when our child is upset and angry, we punish them? No. Anger is also a kind of hurt. Try to soothe and comfort an angry child, too.

20. If we don't give our child some latitude to express themself, they may shut down and talk to us less. Or, they might become more frustrated and even more belligerent in an attempt to be heard and to get their point across.

21. When we introduce a moment of quietness before we say and do something, new ideas can emerge.

Until we introduce a moment of quietness before we say and do something, it will often be the same old thing. Give pause…

22. Black-and-white statements are toxic to a child's developing self-image.

("You're always making a mess!" "You never finish the whole job!" "Why do you always hit your sister?!?!") These messages and the associated energy behind these remarks pollute a child's developing ego, potentially shaping them in a negative way.

23. Every time we slow down and get off cruise control, every time we pause to make sure that what we say and do has some therapeutic value, and every time we intentionally convey love to our child, we are being a conscious parent. It doesn't happen all at once, but it does happen. Just stick with it!

24. Hugging is a good thing. But what if we weren't hugged that much when we were a child? Then, it might not occur to us to hug or to be affectionate. To change this, we must first create a conscious intent like, "I will be more loving by hugging more." Then, we practice, practice, practice on the ones we love.

25. Your child does not have to confide in you. Some kids are naturally private people and prefer to keep things to themself. Others withhold information when Mom and Dad start playing "20 Questions," grilling them for information.

Why not try this?: When a child talks to you, when they spontaneously share something, no matter how mundane, say, "Thanks for sharing that with me."

And sometimes, you might add, "Knowing more about your personal life helps me to feel closer to you, and it also helps me to be a better parent."

Your child helping Mom and Dad to be a better parent? Awesome!

26. Your child's stubbornness is not the problem. It's your child's "misdirected stubbornness" that causes all the problems. This is when a child stubbornly and selfishly goes after what they want without regard for other people's feelings or what is really best for the situation.

Why not try this? The "Oh well" technique (My daughter, Emily, taught me this one).

When Emily turned three, she started fighting us on just about everything. She didn't want to pick up her toys. She didn't want to get her teeth brushed. She didn't want to get in the car seat, and so on. She also wanted to do many things that were just out of the question: Eat ice cream for breakfast, go outside when it was too cold, try to eat all the Pop-Tarts, etc.

Her mom and I decided that as best we could when we asked Emily to do something, we had to make sure that she did it. And when Emily asked us to do something and we told her 'no,' we had to make sure that she wasn't able to turn that initial 'no' into a 'yes.'

And, so it began. This was a difficult phase. Emily would get angry—very angry! Sometimes, I would have to hold her because she would become aggressive or out of control. Emily argued. She pouted and whined. And sometimes, she just went ahead and tried to do something we had already told her not to do.

Then, one day, something interesting happened. I asked Emily to come to the bathroom so we could get her teeth brushed. From her room, she started telling me why it wasn't a good time for her and that I would need to wait. As I was getting up to go to her, *Emily met me in the hallway.* Under her breath, I heard her say, *"Oh well…"*

"Oh well." This was certainly different. Emily and I got those teeth brushed in no time. There was no friction and no negativity.

The therapist in me knew something big had happened. I realized what Emily said wasn't important; what she *didn't say* was important. Emily said, "Oh well," but then I'm convinced she thought something like, "I might as well do it Dad's way because I'm going to have to do it anyway. Oh well."

Emily was beginning to see that fighting her mom and me didn't work. And it was beginning to cost her more than she was willing to pay. Saying "Oh well" also seemed to break down Emily's reactive resistance to instructions and took away her felt need to disagree, argue, and fight. Instead of going toe-to-toe with Mom and Dad, Emily decided to try to cooperate and put herself under our authority.

This is an important milestone, especially for strong-willed kids. This process, where children put themselves under their parents' authority, will always be easiest when we are consistent and carry out our authority with firm and loving-kindness.

27. Conscious parenting isn't just a parenting tool. It's a child-changing, parent-changing, life-changing experience.

28. One reason parents never see and realize the power of positive parenting is they continue to make reactive, negative statements. This waters down, or negates, the power of previously made positive comments.

A child then continues to chase after a parent's praise, or, worse yet; they settle for the devious satisfaction of unconsciously creating a negative drama. A parent can then remain confused and frustrated.

29.

> *People often ask me what is the most effective technique for transforming their life. It's a little embarrassing but after years and years of research and experimentation, I have to say that the answer is just to be a little kinder."*

> — ALDOUS HUXLEY

30. If I took one step forward and then one step back, I would go nowhere. I'm afraid that parenting works the same way.

If we give our child one positive comment for every negative comment, our parenting is balanced, but I'm helping my child go nowhere. This is why parents need to be so cautious when they feel the need to give a child negative feedback. Reframing a less-than-stellar behavior as an improvement over time in the past is much more helpful.

31. Kids mostly behave well. But, if a parent thinks otherwise, they will unconsciously give their child a lot of negative feedback on their not-so-great behavior. A child may then flip, unconsciously trying to match their parent's negative description of them.

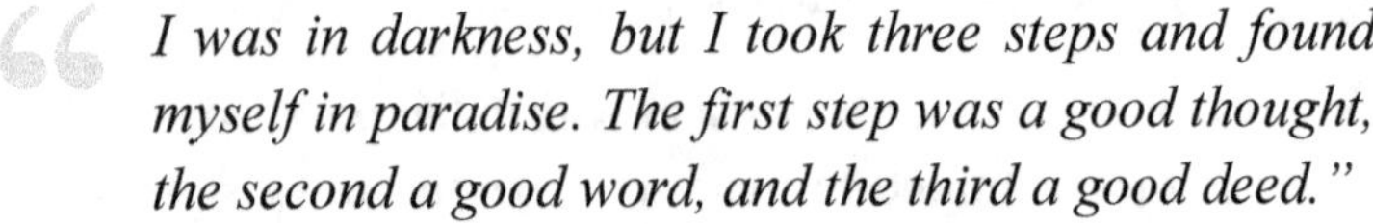

> *I was in darkness, but I took three steps and found myself in paradise. The first step was a good thought, the second a good word, and the third a good deed."*

— FRIEDRICH NIETZSCHE

1. Do you have a conflict or a disagreement? Now, you get to teach your child how you want them to resolve their personal conflicts and disagreements. Kids—they are always watching. Let's give them something conscious to watch.

2. A child who feels appreciated will usually do more than what is expected. And a child who feels unappreciated probably won't.

3. As you become a more conscious parent, the problems don't go away. We just start dealing with them in a better and more conscious way. Then, in all likelihood, problems become less frequent, less severe, and won't last as long.

4. Mistreating a child is always a reflection on the adult. But often, a child personalizes the harshness and begins to think something is wrong with them. They may even start to believe they are "bad," "deserved it," or even that they are "unworthy of love." These messages "stick" and actively drive a child's decision-making well into adulthood.

Psych 101: More times than not, kids aren't aware of what they're thinking. They're thinking; they just don't know *what* they're thinking. But whatever a child says is first a thought. This gives adults a lot of good clues on thought patterns that make children feel bad about themselves—or sad and angry about their life situation.

I teach kids that most of our thoughts are not all that important and that there is nothing to get overly concerned about. When a child believes that their thoughts are important—that they have special meaning—their thoughts will deeply affect them. If this happens, a child will likely try to push away from or block the thoughts they consider to be negative or bad.

Sometimes, during sessions, young people will say the most horrible things about themselves. Kids will say they are "stupid," or "dumb," or they "can't do anything right." "Nobody likes me" is another common phrase I hear. These kids believe they have some character flaw, that something is very wrong with them, or even that their life is cursed.

When a child takes each and every bad thought to heart, they need special instruction, so I go through the following information:

- I remind kids that the stomach digests food, the tear ducts create tears, and the heart pumps blood to every part of our body. Then, I tell them that the brain has a function, too—it thinks. Thinking is just what the brain does. Describing the brain in a purely physiologic way often makes thinking less scary or threatening.
- I ask children if they think too much, too little, or just about the right amount. Every child always answers the same: their mind thinks too much—sometimes way too much! Researchers have discovered that over 95% of our thoughts are repetitive, the same thoughts, over and over and over again. If most of our thinking is the same old stuff, there's really nothing to get that upset about.
- Thoughts that are not observed—those that go in under the radar—do the most harm. But as soon as we observe a thought, as soon as we simply watch it, it doesn't affect us. At that moment, it is just a thought going through our mind, nothing else.
- Kids must learn that the mind often gets things wrong. A child takes in information, but the mind misinterprets it: it just gets things wrong. It's like 2 + 2 somehow becomes equal to 5. Once upon a time, people thought the world

was flat because it looked flat. Because it looked flat, the eyes and the mind made a mistake and assumed that it was flat. Now, that was a big mistake!

If a parent routinely yells at a child, or they are always in trouble, a child may begin to think they are a bad kid. If a teacher takes a critical and harsh approach, a student may begin to think they're dumb or stupid. These messages, and many more like them, become self-descriptors and part of a child's developing self-image. Then a child starts acting out this assigned role without questioning it. It's important to note that these developing beliefs are never true (the mind got it wrong again!), but they become true in the child's mind. These negative thoughts become a bug in a child's mental program—they deeply affect them—but only until they see these messages for what they are and detach from them.

This is when I teach kids simple meditation. As soon as a child can notice just one thought they are having, they make a small dent in their old, conditioned thinking—the thinking that insists they are no good, dumb, stupid or unlovable—any self-descriptor that makes a child feel less important, and less capable than they really are.

Why not try this? There are two general kinds of meditation—active/focused and passive/focused.

Here is one active/focused meditation: You and your child sit comfortably. Each of you picks a focus word (also called a mantra). Make it something simple. Choose a word you don't say very much. Then, try not to say the word at all when it becomes your focus word. In this way, your focus word develops a mystique. It becomes your most "charming thought." Now, your mind will naturally seek it out. With each session, your focus word gains prominence over the barrage of thoughts that give us anxiety and steal our peace. (Note: A mantra can also be a sound like "om" or "ing.")

Now, get settled, close your eyes, and turn inward. Introduce your focus word by saying it silently in your mind. Train your attention on it. Since thinking is so strong, don't be surprised if you are drawn back into your thought stream very quickly. That's completely natural and to be expected.

When you notice that thinking has again taken over, silently reintroduce your focus word and, again, train your attention on it. This pattern will be repeated throughout your meditation session. Remember, this practice is never a waste of time; something important is happening. This meditation 1) helps you see how busy your mind is. Thoughts come fast and furious. 2) slows thoughts and reduces inner tension that unobserved thoughts create. With meditation, you are giving your permission for all your thoughts to come through, so an abnormally busy thought stream slows and begins to normalize. 3) helps you notice a thoughtless space in your mind. This is where inner peace resides —the less thinking, the more inner peace a person will experience.

5. Meditation is the off-ramp for compulsive thinking. Please take the next exit.

6. A child's behavior might initially be annoying. But it doesn't have to stay that way. Step back, and observe…

Now, what do you see? A little boy tapping his pencil instead of doing his homework. A little girl playing with her dolls instead of cleaning her room. A little boy tracking mud into the house once again. In short, you have a kid being a kid. Okay. Now you're ready. No emotional reactivity required.

7. We always have to start from here and now—not from there and later.

8. When a parent devotes themself to their own personal growth and improvement, the whole family benefits.

9. Mindful parenting guards against *mindless* parenting, where we unconsciously hurt our children and sabotage the parent-child relationship.

10. Kids will be wounded by unconscious people. The prevention and cure are the same: love kids well.

> *People heal when they are loved well. If you want to help others heal, love them freely, and without an agenda."*
>
> — ADAPTED FROM A QUOTE BY MIKE
> MCHARGUE

Case Study: A dad recently told me that his mom had raised him to "not take crap from anyone!" He had played this out into his adult life and spent some time in jail for assault.

After his release, Dad unconsciously brought this mindset into his relationship with his 10-year-old son. His son became scared of his dad and afraid to talk to him.

Dad is now trying to do better (and he is). During a recent meeting, he said something in which many parents can identify. He looked at me through tears and raw emotion and said, "When tough is all you know, it's hard to let go."

Yes. Yes, it is. But this dad is right on the cusp of discovering something much better. As the old egoic walls crumble, he is beginning to see the true power of acceptance and vulnerability…

11. Unconscious parents demand respect, "I am the parent! You will respect me! Conscious parents *command* respect. They carry out their authority with compassionate firmness and integrity. At some level, children appreciate this approach and are more likely to respond positively.

12. Children are so sensitive. They take in and absorb what parents feel. And our words and actions reflect how we feel. If we're angry, kids absorb anger. If we're nervous, they absorb our nervousness, and so on.

This is why nothing is more important than discovering our inner peace and activating our intention to love. Then, children will absorb our love and peacefulness, which is just what every kid needs.

13. When someone hurts us or makes us angry, those feelings squeeze out and momentarily replace the love we have for them. Or, we could say that the angry feelings (driven by hurt) "pin love down," like in a wrestling match. At these times, love cannot influence our decision-making. We have been cut off from love! I think you would agree that this can be a dangerous time for anyone!

But, if we think about what the other person truly means to us, if we reintroduce the intention to love, if we become open and allow uncomfortable feelings to pass, the love begins to return, slowly squeezing out the hurt and angry feelings. Or we could say that love is able to "break free" from the hold of anger and hurt. With love back in charge, what we say and do will reflect that love, calm the situation, and have a true therapeutic value.

14. When we tell a child what they must do to solve a problem, we take away an important opportunity for them to learn how to be a good problem solver.

It's their problem. Let them own it. Guide them. Help them. Support them. Offer information. But whenever possible, let them struggle with their problems so they can come up with their own solutions.

Why not try this? There are many types of yogic breathing, and I'm absolutely sure all of them are helpful because when we control our breathing, we are breathing consciously, not unconsciously. For most of us, stress dominates our breathing—until we notice what's happening and take our breathing back. (Insert big sigh here.)

Perhaps the simplest breathing technique is "following the breath." Here, you simply notice the breath coming in and then notice the breath going out. You focus on and begin to notice all of the muscles involved with an inhalation. You hold your breath briefly at the top of the in-breath and relax your tummy. Then, you let your breath out slowly. (Note: Counting while doing this exercise gives your mind something to do instead of thinking so much.) Also, counting as you breathe gives you a rough measurement of how long you can extend your full breath (some yogis can make a breath last well over one minute!) Then there is the bonus of less thinking!

A second popular breathing technique is called "square breathing." There are some excellent videos on the internet to teach your child this method. But, as soon as they are able, you want to help them internalize this technique so they can take square breathing with them wherever they go. Then, a young person can use square breathing when they want to feel calmer and more centered in their body.

Another helpful breathing technique is what I call "the stabilizing breath." To begin, sit in a comfortable chair. Lean back and cross your arms. Lock your arms so that when you relax them, they stay in place. Now breathe in and watch how your forearm moves out from your chest. Hold your breath for 3 to 4 seconds. Then, as slowly as possible, let your breath out. For this breath, counting is again helpful. Stay with this exercise until anxiety lessens and calmness returns. I have seen many kids with panic attacks use this technique, and in a short time, their panic was no longer such a problem for them.

15. I recently watched some parents with their three young children. Every time they would say a child's name it was to tell them to stop doing something or to give them some other directive. I think when kids hear their name, they should anticipate a word of praise or another positive exchange, not just a reprimand or instruction.

16. My kids sometimes make me feel worried, angry, upset, and disappointed. Sometimes, it is therapeutic for them (and me) to tell them how their behavior makes me feel. I do this carefully with no attempt to control or to lay a guilt trip on them.

17. A child who is not respected by his parents will not have true respect for anyone, including themself.

18. Unbridled criticism and harshness make the light go out in a child's eyes as they become discouraged. Or a child may get angry and go into "fighting mode."

But when we parent consciously, we are tuned in and sensitive to our child's inner state. Discouragement does not motivate kids to change. And anger will only magnify the initial problem.

19. Some parents try to assert authority but totally forget the importance of earning respect. We earn respect by how well we exercise and carry out our authority over our children.

20. You cannot punish and consequence a child into good behavior.

Helping a child change negative behavior while helping them build positive behavior patterns, takes a high degree of conscious awareness. For best results, focus on the good or improved behavior that is already there.

Why not try this? Teach your child a yoga breath called "Darth Vader breathing" (also known as *ujjayi pranayama* in Sanskrit, which means "the victorious breath.") With Darth Vader breathing, you draw in your breath over the larynx or voice box so it makes a noise (it sounds a little like a prolonged, light snore). You do the out-breath the same way. With Darth Vader breathing, the in-breath and the out-breath are always under some degree of pressure, which creates the noise. Go ahead. Take a moment to play around with it…

Okay. The beauty of this breath is that it is easier to control a breath when you can both feel the breath and *hear the breath*. You might also notice it is easier to prolong this breathing technique, so you are able to extend your breath for a longer time. The big bonus feature of Darth Vader's breathing is that it's much harder for the overly busy mind to break in and distract us from doing this exercise.

After you teach your child Darth Vader breathing, play a short board game. Play the game while everyone engages in Darth Vader's breathing. Participants try to lightheartedly catch other players who forget to breathe this way. No pressure. Just fun!

Getting in touch with our breath and focusing on our heartbeat immediately takes us away from thinking. It also puts us on the fast track to being centered and grounded in our bodies.

21. Parents want results! We want our kids to change a behavior, stop a behavior, or improve a behavior. Unfortunately, our impatience—in the form of frustration—is absorbed by a child, which often slows their progress. Plus this state of impatience keeps us from conveying love, the biggest catalyst for change there is.

22. Here are two reasons timeouts often do not work: 1) parents put too much energy into the timeout through heated, intense, negative interactions, and 2) parents haven't established enough positive, energized relationship time, so the child unconsciously settles for the negative attention they receive through the time out. Paraphrased from a blog by Howard Glasser, co-author of Transforming the Difficult Child.

23. Consistently convey love. Don't leave this important task to chance. Otherwise, your child might get the wrong idea. They may begin to think it's more about their good behavior and pleasing their parents—instead of the child knowing, at a deep level, that they are loved and valued just the way they are.

24. If we constantly tell a child what to do, they might become dependent on that level of direction. If we prompt a child indirectly, they will quickly learn to monitor their behavior.

Example: *"We have to leave for school in 30 minutes. What do you need to do to be ready on time?"* or *"Bedtime is in 10 minutes. What else do you have to do to be ready for bed?"*

25. Detachment is easily misunderstood. Detachment doesn't mean you care or love less. It means you aren't as affected and thrown off by the psychological pushes and pulls that are present in all heavy, emotional interactions.

26. To be a conscious parent, all we have to do is slow down and remember one thing: Our child has feelings, too.

27. A great Conscious Parenting principle is: Give credit where credit is due.

Why not try this? Following directions with a bad attitude is still following directions. The unconscious parent focuses on the child's bad attitude. However, the conscious parent focuses on the self-discipline the child used to start a task they didn't really want to do. In this way, there's more effort and follow-through as a child's bad attitude melts away.

If a child cleans their room but doesn't clean it all that well, a parent can start with a loud, critical remark. Or, with more conscious awareness, they can give credit where credit is due: mention a few things the child did or one or two things they did well—then nicely ask them to do the one or two things they missed.

28. If you want to know the health of an organization, don't talk to the management; talk to the employees.

So, if you want to know the health of a family, talk to your kids. Ask them how you're doing. Ask them if they think you are fair. And be sure to ask them if they have any doubts about how much you love them.

29. When parents are always trying to "keep their child in line," the unspoken message the child receives is that we don't believe they can make good decisions for themself. Strategic positive cuing—pointing out naturally occurring positive behaviors—is a much better way to go.

30. Corporal punishment is sometimes the unconscious thought, "My child is misbehaving. I will hurt them. Then they will stop." Sounds harsh, right? But what else would drive us to hit our kids?

In contrast, Conscious Parenting is the conscious thought, "My child is misbehaving. I will try to understand, be patient with them, and try to help them. And I will be open and honest with my feelings so I can keep my words and actions from making things worse."

We work to consciously become the kind of person (and parent) we decide to be—or Life's hardships, in conjunction with our unconscious mind, will dictate the kind of person we become."

— JAY MORGAN

JULY

1. When your child is belligerent, don't freak out! They are practicing assertiveness, a critically important life skill. At these tense times, disengage. Your job is to help your child temper their strong words and emotions—not to squash them.

2. Usually, the more a person says they don't care, the more they really care. Usually, they mean, "I don't want to care! When I care, it upsets me. And I don't want to be upset."

Whenever I don't care, I constrict my feelings. Then, I become less sensitive and aware of them. At the same time, I become less sensitive and aware of other people's feelings. So, increased feelings of separateness and callousness towards others are the natural result of not caring.

3. You don't help a child grow up to "be somebody." You help them to grow up with the knowledge and assurance that they already are.

4. The more a parent fails to relinquish the need for control, the more a strong-willed child will assert their autonomy in an unhealthy way. These negative behaviors become messages to a parent that they can't, and shouldn't try to control their child's life. Remember to work *with* children, not *on* them.

5. Don't waste your time trying to "make a child be good." Focus instead on conveying love, practicing good communication, and building a spirit of cooperation. Your child will do the rest.

6. Children who feel cherished by their parents rarely have any serious self-esteem issues.

7. Focusing on your child to the point where there is only you and there is only them is the ultimate self-esteem builder.

8. The person devoted to self-healing is more conscious in their dealings with others. The unhealed person does the best they can but tends to lash out at others whenever they feel threatened; whenever they sense someone getting too close to their "stuff," their suppressed emotional pain.

Case Study: Nine-year-old Chloe is being raised by her aunt and uncle. Tragically, her mom died of an overdose, and her birth father is a drug-dealing sociopath who gave up his parental rights.

Along with grief work, I will occasionally bring up the subject of her dad just to see where she's at on this issue and to give her an opportunity to talk. In response to a recent query, Chloe responded, "Dad? Oh, I don't give him my thoughts."

Dad turned his back on Chloe, and her response was to *not give him a place in her mind*—to not give him her thoughts. Brilliant Chloe! Thanks for the conscious reminder on how to deal with past hurts.

(Chloe's nonchalant remark, "Dad? Oh, I don't give him my thoughts," made it clear she is not suppressing a painful issue but "mentally sliding past it," preferring to keep her attention trained on what's happening in the now moment. In this way, her sad story from the past doesn't become a lifelong burden.)

9. When you win an argument with your child, you may lose something much greater—closeness.

10. Your positive attention is the lifeline to your child's positive behavior. (Note: You might want to read this one twice.)

11. Recipe for helping a child be motivated: 1) Make encouraging comments, and 2) refrain from making discouraging comments. Your child will do the rest.

12. A child can draw you into a head-to-head conflict, or you can consciously draw them into a heart-to-heart relationship.

Why not try this? When you are angry or upset and a child is around, why not say, "I've been upset or mad long enough. I'm going to let this go." Then, when your child is upset or angry, you can encourage them to let it go, too.

You can even write what you want to let go of on a piece of paper, wad it up and drop it. Encourage your child to do the same thing when they are upset about something. Keep the wadded-up paper around so a child can see all of the seemingly important things that upset them that they learned to drop.

But dropping other things is a mistake. With many situations, kids need to dig in to solve a life challenge. Use another sheet of paper titled, "Life Challenge Worksheet" to facilitate this exercise in logic and planning.

13. When we pause—when we do not reactively meet a child's resistance with adult resistance—that is not weakness but a demonstration of great self-control and inner strength. Conscious responses can then find their way to you.

14. Conscious parents keep their cool even in the heat of the moment. Yelling at kids is the psychological equivalent of putting a drop of poison in their oatmeal. Uncontrolled anger is toxic to the system, especially little systems.

15. How about those kids that don't fit any mold; the ones that march to a completely different drummer, to music no one else can hear? These kids can be tricky and difficult, but can take us places we never even imagined.

16. I don't care how many letters you have after your name, how many people you supervise, or how full your schedule might be. If a toddler hands you a toy phone, you darn well better answer it!

Don't be too busy or too important to miss an opportunity to connect with your children.

Why not try this? Here are some examples of the second type of meditation: passive/focused.

Sit with your child in a quiet place. Close your eyes and just breathe. Don't try to manipulate your breath; just casually notice how you are breathing, without any judgment like, *"I need to breathe more fully,"* or *"I need to slow my breath down."* When you just observe your breathing, notice how it slows down and normalizes on its own. Try this exercise multiple times a day, even if it's just for one breath.

Sit with your child in a quiet place. Close your eyes. Silently, tell yourself, *"My next thought is..."* Be alert. Wait in silence until you become aware of your next thought. Then, let that thought go and wait for the next. When you're thinking mind again takes over, it's back to your centering breath, and to your prompt: *"My next thought is..."*

Repeat this process until the end of your meditation. Watching a thought neutralizes it and expands one's conscious awareness.

A simpler version which you can do almost anywhere, is to blink one time whenever you notice that you're thinking. It is important to realize that when we disrupt a conditioned thought pattern (one of our old thought patterns that too narrowly and inadequately defines us), it weakens and begins to dissolve. When an old egoic thought structure begins to dissolve, our higher self can resurface. And meditation can provide the opening...

17. When a child is acting "too big for their britches," do they really need a parent to "cut them down to size?"

18. Parents who try to control kids leave kids with few options. Strong-willed kids will usually do some unhealthy thing to show a parent they can't run their life. Other children will begin to cave in and become more dependent on, and subservient to, the controlling parent.

The fix? Remember that control is an illusion. Be aware of your subconscious efforts to try to control. And most importantly, acknowledge and honor a child's free will. Work *with* children, not *on* them.

19. Conscious parents are always trying to work themselves out of a job. They strategically parent so their children will grow up and be able to "parent themselves." As adults, they will then be able to responsibly tell themselves what to do, and what not to do, so they can secure a happy future and a fulfilling life. To accomplish this, conscious parents often ask themselves, "Right now, how can I do less so that my child can do more?"

Trying to answer this question will lead a parent to a response that will foster more independence and less dependence in their child.

Why not try this? When a child acts out, try to credibly present this message: "Your behavior is not okay, but it is an improvement (over a specific time or similar incident in the past). In Conscious Parenting, this is called a reframe—presenting information to a child in a way that suggests they are doing better.

(Example: "Yelling at your sister is not okay, but I noticed that you stopped yourself and didn't push her like last week. That is much better self-control. Thanks for working on that! Now that you're calmer, do you think you can tell your sister what you wanted to say without yelling?")

Since this communication is encouraging, a child listens and continues to try harder to change. This message also builds optimism so that a child feels they can do even better in the future. In contrast, critical statements create pessimism where a child feels discouraged and may start to think they will never get things right.

When we give direction or feedback to our children, there will be an inner "yes" or an inner "no." If we present information in a conscious way, a child will have an inner "yes." This means they will be more likely to hear us and consider what we are saying. If we present information in an unconscious way, a child will have an inner "no." Then, they might close down or go into fight-or-flight mode.

20. Many children tend to be egocentric and self-absorbed.

Parents help children to be more thoughtful by noticing and commenting on their small attempts at thoughtfulness—not by going on and on about their perceived *thoughtlessness*. And parents help a child be more sensitive to the feelings of others by noticing their small attempts at being sensitive—not by going on and on about their perceived *insensitivity*.

21. Parents have a "map in their head" of how they think they need to parent. It is usually made up of the "old stuff," a combination of how they were parented as a child—both the good and the bad. That's why conscious parents consult the old map but change it as needed so their parenting is dynamic, sensible, and effective.

22. We are changing all the time. The goal is to change consciously and not let the stuff in our unconscious mind keep us fearful and stuck in the same place.

Psych 101: "My child seems to actually enjoy getting in trouble."

Many parents don't understand how a child could possibly feel good about getting negative attention. For many strong-willed kids, creating a negative drama gives them a feeling of power and control. For others, it serves as a diversion, momentarily taking their attention away from an inner state where they are experiencing uncomfortable feelings.

Why not try this? Many parents say, "My kids never get along! They fight all the time!" This statement is never true, but that doesn't matter because it is *true to the parent*. The only thing the parent sees is the children not getting along and the children always fighting.

For Conscious Parenting to begin, a parent has to notice the children getting along, getting along better, not arguing as much, not arguing as loudly, or practicing enough self-control not to let things get physical. Then, a parent makes these behaviors the focus of their attention and gives their children feedback that reflects these exciting improvements. As a parent initiates this process, they may find themself rubbing their eyes and thinking, "Where did all this positive behavior come from?" when it was there all along, just out of their field of vision.

23. It stands to reason that if a parent routinely overreacts to a child's behavior, the child will learn to overreact to minor stressors in their life. In other words, parental overreacting can easily contribute to a child developing problems with emotional dysregulation.

24. The best way to talk to a child about a negative behavior is in terms of the progress they have made on improving that behavior.

25. Unconscious parenting can be like putting out fires, rushing from one behavior problem to the next. In contrast, conscious parents have a plan. They are not reactive. They continually keep in mind what they are trying to teach and instill in their children. They use Conscious Parenting principles, enthusiastically commenting on their child's desirable behavior while dialing back their energy when addressing their child's undesirable behavior.

26. Conscious parents know the importance of uninterrupted listening. Parents ask questions to clarify a point, and they reflect back what was said so a child feels heard and understood.

When this work is done, it's not unusual for a child to pause and say, "Dad, what do you think?" Then, a parent will be completely ready to share, and a child will be completely ready to listen. If we aren't listening well, everything else will be off too.

27. A formula for Conscious Parenting: When your child is engaging in a negative behavior:

1. Wait.
2. Mentally accept the misbehavior.
3. Acknowledge and accept your associated feelings, and let them pass.
4. Watch and listen to what you would have said or done if you had reacted emotionally.
5. Trust that the perfect response will come to you. Then proceed.

28. Parents earn respect by how well they exercise their authority over a child. If a parent is compassionate but firm, a child may not like every decision a parent makes. Still, they will be more accepting of those decisions, less angry, and more cooperative.

Why not try this? When a child asks if they can do something, try not to make a snap decision. Even if it's a good decision, if we make it too quickly, a child will often react negatively. Instead, take your time. "Wrestle" with a decision. Talk to your partner. Ask a child for more information. Then, when you tell your child of your decision, they know it was not a snap decision, and they will probably be less reactive and more acceptant.

29. Many parents are super sensitive to their children's distress. They don't like their child to be sad, angry, and upset, so they try to "make it all better." They try to alleviate their child's emotional discomfort.

But sometimes, a child is upset because of a decision they made—a decision that brought on a consequence or a real-life hardship. While parents should refrain from saying, "You should have listened to me!" they do need to allow this kind of suffering to be there. This helps the child to see that their stress and emotional pain are of their own making and could have been avoided. Too much comfort and consoling dilutes this critically important message.

30. Consciousness is contagious. The farther you go with your Conscious Parenting, the harder it will be for your child (and partner) to continue to behave unconsciously. Stay at it. Consciousness will always win… one way or another.

31. Some people have egos that regularly need angry energy to make them feel complete. If we refuse to argue and fight with a person who has an angry ego, they will:

1. Intensify their efforts to draw us into a fight.
2. Stop and walk away in frustration.
3. Pick a fight with someone else.
4. Or maybe, just maybe, calm down and begin to discuss a point of disagreement. And yes, this works with children and teenagers, too.

AUGUST

1. If we are going to give a kid "a piece of our mind," let's make sure it's a piece of our conscious mind, not our unconscious mind.

Reactive comment? Probably unconscious. Responsive comment after a pause? Definitely conscious.

2. Parents love doing nice things for their kids, and they love getting them nice things. But how much is too much? When kids fail to show appreciation or begin to act entitled (acting as if they deserve something, and they get angry or terribly sad when they don't immediately get it), a parent is likely doing too much.

> *I don't mind spoiling my kids as long as my kids don't act spoiled."*

> — JAY MORGAN

3. It seems as if many parents rely on criticism to induce change, when my experience suggests that positive feedback works much better.

If a parent becomes adept at noticing all the opportunities to affirm their child and build them up through positive feedback, a child's sense of self is more healthy and positive. This means a child will be more immune to unbridled criticism and negativity from unconscious people. And when a parent is adept at affirming their child and giving them positive feedback, when they have to make a corrective statement, it will come from a place of love, not from any desire for control.

4. Most of our frustration comes from our preconceived notions of what we think our child's behavior should be like at a given moment—what we think they should be doing, or what we think they should not be doing. When we drop these preconceived notions and just be with and deal with our child openly, in the now moment, our frustration will be much more manageable.

5. Some people mistakenly believe that love and hate are feelings when, in my experience, they are actually decisions we make. A person can make us furiously angry or hurt us badly, but they cannot make us hate them. Hate is our personal choice.

In a similar way, we can have positive and affectionate feelings toward someone. Still, they can't make us love them because this most important decision always comes from ourselves (The exception is romantic love, which is a wonderful feeling state, but for the most part, effortless).

6. Conscious Parenting would be easier if we felt unconditional love for our children all the time, which, of course, we don't. But true unconditional love has little to do with feelings. It is a highly conscious, volitional act of our will. And the highest form of unconditional love involves sharing and channeling love from our higher self, not the ego.

Psych 101: Some parents feel bad or think they must be doing something wrong when they don't feel love for their kids all the time—or when they feel intense anger or resentment. In these instances, a parent is attempting the impossible: they are trying to control their feelings. They tell themselves they should feel this way, and they should not feel that way, instead of just being in touch with the thoughts and feelings they are experiencing.

When we tune into our feelings, we quickly realize we do not have positive feelings toward our children all the time—and that's okay. It's normal. The main thing is how we treat our children, not how we feel towards them. When we accept this truth, there is nothing to suppress, and there's nothing to feel guilty about. Parenting is hard enough without mentally beating ourselves up for something we really can't control.

7. Child: "How are you able to be such a good dad to me when grandpa had so many problems?"

Dad: "I just gave you all the things that I longed for from my dad —things he couldn't or was not able to give me."

8. An unconscious parent's mindset: *"I'll say what I want, and I'll do what I want. I'm the parent!"*

A Conscious Parent's mindset: *"I'll say what I want, and I'll do what I want, but with thoughtfulness and compassion."*

9. When a parent snaps at a child, the child will not, in all likelihood, say, "Daddy, please don't talk to me that way," so I will speak to parents for them.

When a parent smacks a belligerent teen in the mouth, the teen will probably not have the wherewithal to say, "When you slap me, it hurts and makes me feel furious and disrespected. I have strong feelings about this, and I wish you would just listen," so I will speak to parents for them.

When a preschooler asks a parent to play and is repeatedly told, "No," they will probably not have the words to say, "I love you, Mommy, but when you don't play, it makes me question your love for me," so I will speak to parents for them.

10. When they were younger, I regularly pulled my daughters aside and asked them how I was doing as a parent. At first, each of the girls would respond by acting silly, refusing to take the question seriously, or dismissing me with, "Oh fine, Dad."

But with persistence and more specific questions, such as, "Do you think I am being fair?" "Am I a good listener?" and "Do you ever question how much I love you?" I have obtained some very useful information.

My goal is to be a great parent to my kids, not just in my mind.

11. The better your relationship with your partner, the better your relationship with your kids. Consider doing whatever you need to do so you and your partner are on the same page and negative emotions don't build up.

12. Parents will necessarily have to label behaviors as "good" or "bad." But be very careful. Too many "bad behavior messages" can make a child begin to question their inherent goodness. This can lead to more negative behavior as a child starts acting out a role they feel they have been assigned.

13. Instead of asking a child for a hug, be sure to mix it up by asking if you can give your child a hug. Love is about receiving, but love is mostly about giving. And as always, parents must lead by example.

14. Selfishness is usually bad, but not always. Healthy selfishness is not neglecting yourself and not leaving yourself out of the equation. Healthy selfishness is knowing yourself and doing the things you must do so that you can be at your best—for your partner and your kids. Healthy selfishness is love for self and love for others in balance. In that way, everyone wins.

15. From *The Conscious Parenting Dictionary:*

- MIND READING (verb): A nasty habit where a parent assumes they know why their child said or did something. Then, the parent, usually in a bold and brash tone, proceeds to tell their child why they said or did something with no real objective basis—just opinion and conjecture.

Mind reading is a surefire way to build resentment, tension, and distance in the parent-child relationship.

- EXPLORING (verb): A way of questioning a child that focuses on helping the parent understand possible motives behind their child's behavior. Exploring is a surefire way to build cooperation, closeness, and mutual respect in the parent-child relationship.

Why not try this? Good impulse control is taking the time to make sure that what a person wants to say or do is a good idea—something that is necessary, kind, and helpful.

Tell your child that you're going to say a phrase. Their job is to hold the phrase in their mind for a moment and not automatically say it back. (Example: "The sky seems very blue today," or "I like to wear comfy clothes.") Then, when you say okay, the child is to say the phrase back to you. Parents can start with a simple phrase and make it longer as a child progresses.

In the next phase of this exercise, a parent will give their child a simple instruction like, "Raise your right hand" or "Clap your hands two times." The same rule applies: your child is to hold the instruction on what to do in their mind until the parent says okay. Then, the child is to act on the instruction that was given. Parents can start with a one-part instruction and then, as a child is able, advance to a two, three, or even four-part instruction. (Example: Stand up. Put your hands over your head. Touch your toes, then sit down.)

When children pause and wait, they exercise the part of their brain that can screen information and evaluate if something is a good idea or a bad idea. With this exercise, a child is one step away from being able to evaluate their own thoughts and impulses. This simple practice helps kids make sure that what they say and do is a good idea, not something that will needlessly upset someone or get them in trouble.

16. Before they learn differently, strong-willed kids actively look for two things: power and control. These children can obtain an unhealthy satisfaction by drawing their parents into an argument, wearing them down so an initial 'no' becomes a 'yes,' or sneakily going behind a parent's back to break a rule or disregard an instruction.

Conscious parents must be aware of this propensity and guide their children into developing self-control and exercising power, not over others, but over their unhealthy and self-serving decision-making.

17. A "check-up from the neck up" is important for all of us. This is when we look at our thoughts and try to understand why we said or did something. But also, don't forget about the "check-up from the neck down." This is understanding and being in touch with our body—any physical sensations or emotional feelings we may be having. Then, we can learn how to relax into a stressful situation, express our feelings assertively, or perhaps just let them run their course. This is also an important step in Conscious Parenting.

18. Children understanding sex is like a youngster putting together a 5000-piece puzzle. They will start on the border pieces and then gradually work toward tackling the really tough and tricky inner pieces. Needless to say, it will be a difficult process that will take a long time.

On this "sex puzzle," parents need to provide information when needed to make sure a child does not get stuck and finishes putting together the puzzle. This helps ensure children and teens understand and develop a more complete picture of this critically important life issue.

Case Study: Eight-year-old Thomas burst into the kitchen and asked his mom, "Where did I come from?" His mom looked up. She knew this day would come. Mom got out her books and diagrams and started to go over everything—intercourse, conception, how a baby develops in the womb, and birth. When she finished, she looked over at her son, who had his mouth open, seemingly in mild shock. Mom asked if he had any questions. Thomas looked at her and seemed a bit disoriented. He shook his head. "No," Thomas said. "My friend Scott said he was from Oklahoma, and that made me wonder where I came from."

This is a funny story that illustrates an important point: Find out what is behind a child's question before you answer it. Then, only provide the information they need to answer the question and satisfy their curiosity. Don't burden a child with information for which they may not be ready.

19. When you're angry, Plan A will likely suck. It could be full of anger or an unconscious desire to control. When you're angry, you often have to go to Plan B, or sometimes Plan C, or even Plan D—as many plans as you need to make sure that what you say and do will help and serve to calm a tense situation.

20. A child is not a "tabula rasa"—a blank slate. A child is more like soft clay, to be held gently and artfully molded.

21. Keep reading to a child. Keep reading with a child. Keep searching until you find that one book that hooks a child on reading. Parents can breathe a little easier when their child develops a love for reading.

> *Reading is the gateway skill that makes all other learning possible."*

— BARACK OBAMA

22.

> *I would rather have questions that can't be answered than answers that can't be questioned."*

— RICHARD FEYNMAN

Why not try this? Maybe your child helped with something but did so reluctantly or with a negative attitude. But still, they *did* help. At bedtime, why not say, "Thanks again for helping me with (the task). I appreciate your help." Or, "Today, you didn't want to help me with (the task), but you did anyway. You didn't have the best attitude, but I still really appreciate your help."

23. Everyone carries a certain amount of emotional pain around with them, children included. When your teenager snaps at you, try not to take it personally. Their snappiness is only a symptom of the old emotions they have suppressed or the thoughts and feelings they are inwardly experiencing. In these situations, a parent's detachment is crucial.

24. Forgive, and you're free to love again. Don't forgive, and you're not.

Why not try this? Forgiveness is a decision we make, and then we back it up with kind words and actions. We don't have to feel like being kind to be kind. Or, I might feel like yelling at someone, but I don't have to yell at them. These are my decisions. For example, I can smile at someone and say, "Good morning," no matter how I feel toward them. So, for the forgiveness process to work, we have to act as if we have already forgiven a person until our feelings soften toward them. This is another aspect of unconditional love.

25. By their nature, positive behaviors are more subtle than negative behaviors, so if we're not careful, we'll miss them… until we train ourselves not to.

26. Spoken words have a message. And every spoken message has an energy or a 'vibe.' Are we giving out positive energy and good vibrations today?

27. Really listening to your child and asking questions; really listening to your child and reflecting information; refraining from jumping in and making a premature remark—all of this works to make a child think, *"Wow! Dad wants to know me and understand what I think and how I feel. He really cares."*

28. Unconditional love is intentionally engaging in loving actions, even when we don't feel it—even when no feelings of love are present. Unconditional love is also developing enough self-discipline not to react negatively when we're being disrespected or mistreated, allowing the negative energy to move through us and not coming back with anything negative. Make no mistake—that is love, too.

29. Trying to control kids will be like force-feeding a grizzly bear or trying to push a rope. Connect through positivity and build a spirit of cooperation instead.

30. A mental expectation can be a veiled desire or attempt to control. Make an expectation a preference instead. If you expect your child to take out the trash and they don't, you will probably have a strong reaction. But preferring that a child take out the trash is softer thinking. Then, when they don't, emotions will not run so high. This technique helps us restructure our thoughts so as to avoid mental rigidity, which directly causes strong emotional reactions.

31. Misbehaving is a miss on behaving well—nothing more, and nothing less. Parents can't afford to take it personally. Then, they'll lose their edge and start reacting, possibly even reinforcing and strengthening the negative behavior they are trying to help a child change.

1. Some parents tell me their child seems to enjoy pushing their buttons and making them upset. And they are often right. Strong-willed kids actively look for power and control. Button pushing is both. The strong-willed child can come to believe that they have the power to make a parent lose their cool and control them by making them so angry.

The Fix? Allow your child to help you locate all your buttons—and then disconnect them. Let go of what would have been your emotional reaction and wait for a conscious response.

2. Imagine that you are taking a walk with your child. As you walk together, holding hands and talking, you lead them on a beautiful path through the park. This is a great word picture of how to work with children. Because of the closeness and quality of communication and because of the love being conveyed, a child stays with you. A parent can then lead their child on a safe path until they are ready to set out on their own.

3.

Anger is sadness's bodyguard."

— LIZA PALMER

When a child is sad, sometimes they are more comfortable being angry. Once a child's anger has passed, you might ask them if something was making them angry *and sad*. This question can educate and get to the real heart of the matter.

Why not try this? *"Am I naughty—or nice?"* Your child is always in the process of answering this important question. They will listen and take in their parents' spoken and unspoken messages and allow these messages to shape them. Some parents reactively provide frequent and intense feedback when a child messes up, leading them to question their goodness. But, when a child makes a good decision, it is often overlooked or addressed generically with feigned exuberance (Good job!) Be conscious. Make a compelling and convincing case that your child is good, makes good decisions, or is on the verge of overcoming a negative behavior pattern.

4.

> *Once we believe in ourselves, we can risk curiosity, wonder, spontaneous delight, or any experience that reveals the human spirit."*
>
> — E. E. CUMMINGS

Cummings is describing a world that is not available to most adults. But this is the natural world of a young child. Little kids are bold and curious and experience moment after moment "spontaneous delight." It's easy for them to believe in themselves because they only have one self. Their ego hasn't fully developed yet.

I believe this is what Jesus meant when he said that we must "become like little children" if we want to enter the kingdom of heaven. In other words, we must take measures to transcend the ego so we can recapture this world of curiosity, wonder, and spontaneous delight.

5. Conscious Parents use strategic interventions to keep things going right—and to prevent things from going wrong. And when things do go wrong, they use more strategic interventions to help things start to go right again.

6. Conscious Parents are proactive. They are pros at not acting until they are sure what they want to say and do will help a situation—and not make things worse.

7. Flattery will get you nowhere. But neither will criticism and negativity. Try praise, encouragement, affirming comments, and shaping positive behavior instead.

Why not try this? Not all encouraging comments are created equal. Let's compare the following statements:

"You can get a hit! I just know it!" is nice for a child to hear, but it may not be enough to drown out their own thoughts of self-doubt.

"I know you can get a hit! You've been practicing so hard, and you hit so many balls in practice! You've got this!"

When you're giving a child an encouraging comment, be ready to back it up by elaborating on a success or an improvement from the recent past.

8. Sadly, some parents have what I call a "better than ego." Unconsciously, they need to feel better and more important than others, even their children. These parents say and do things that put them (their ego) in a one-up position while putting their child in a one-down position. This can leave a child feeling confused and insecure.

Why not try this? When you're helping a child tame their anger, don't just tell them what they can't do when they're mad; tell them what they *can do*. This helps ensure that anger is released and not suppressed, where it can cause more problems later.

Default Anger Plan:

- Push-ups and a plank. As soon as a child gets angry, muscles in their arms and hands will start getting tight. These exercises release that tension quickly.
- Repeatedly scream into a pillow. Screaming releases anger directly. It is similar to how crying releases sadness directly.
- Jumping jacks or running in place. These exercises create an aerobic workout, release angry energy, and usually take some of the fight out of an angry episode. Multiple reps can even bring on some fatigue.

Ask a child to count the pushups, jumping jacks, and number of screams into the pillow. They can also count the seconds they hold a plank or run in place. Counting distracts their mind and helps them escape from angry thinking.

Anger creates irrational thinking, and many times, when a child gets angry, they will refuse to do their anger plan. For best results, have a child practice their anger plan daily *before they get angry.*

9. A parent's feedback can be positive, neutral, or negative. Kids prefer positive feedback—the message that a parent likes or is happy with their behavior. Then, the child comes to see—often with help—that healthy behaviors "feel better" than unhealthy ones. Over time, this is internalized where a child does "good" not to please anyone, but because they prefer it.

10. Conscious Parents make conscious statements, which become an invitation for children to join them, communicating and interacting on a more conscious level as well.

11. A child will do best when we tell them what they are doing right or what they are improving on. Wouldn't everyone?

Case Study: Eve came home from college for the weekend. She started telling her mom and dad about the changes she needed to make: more exercise, working more efficiently, and trying to get her days and nights back the way they were supposed to be. At this point, Eve's dad almost said, "…and you could also do this, and this, and this."

But, thankfully, he stopped himself. Dad realized a comment like that would be very discouraging and would probably anger Eve. She might even think that her dad believed she wasn't doing all that well at college. (Her GPA at the time was 3.8) Instead, Dad was able to say, "Those are great ideas!"

This illustrates another important principle of Conscious Parenting: The first thing you want to say is often the last thing you need to say.

12. Why do even Conscious Parents need so many reminders to keep things positive? Because we live in a critical and fault-finding world. But we can change that, beginning with our family.

13. In a disagreement, it will take two people to keep the peace. In a conflict, it will take two people to rediscover the peace. However, if one party doesn't seem to want to keep the peace—or rediscover the peace—a person will have to rely on their own inner peace. Then, they will know how to proceed.

14. "Do this!" "Don't do that!" "Not that way! Do it this way!"

Parental overcorrection is a nasty habit. All these statements say, "You failed," and create a breeding ground for anger and resentment. Emphasizing a child's positive behavior choices, reframing a negative behavior as an improvement, and giving plenty of affirming comments is a much better way to go.

Why not try this? If a child tries to aggravate a sibling, a conscious parent might say, "It looks like you want Sara to notice you. But instead of being nice, you grabbed her doll and threw it down. Can you come up to her again and ask if you can play too? Or if she wants to play something else with you?"

Then, praise any effort. Also, be sure to ask the child which way made them feel best and which way helped them feel closer to their sister.

15. Scolding and reactive criticism make the conscious parent feel superior to their child and their child feel less important. It is a relationship killer.

16. Every time you learn something about Conscious Parenting, you add another tool to your tool belt. But these tools don't weigh you down; they empower you.

17. Inner strength and outer loudness are opposites and mutually exclusive. Inner strength is an attempt to control one's self, while outer loudness is an attempt to control another person—or to just dump anger on them.

18. Expressions of love can "clean up the mess" made by unconscious words and actions. It also kicks off the forgiveness process and has a softening effect on hard feelings.

19. If we do small things—washing our hands, chopping vegetables, walking up stairs, etc.—with a lot of conscious awareness, it helps us be more prepared for parenting with more conscious awareness, too.

20. When working with a child who is misbehaving, Conscious Parents keep their centeredness and, in that way, they never lose their love.

21. Conscious Parents need to clearly give children the game rules: "Don't jump on the furniture," "Always tell the truth," "Keep your room clean," and so on. Then, parents train themselves to notice when a child remembers a rule, follows a rule, improves on following a rule, or when a length of time goes by when a child has not broken a rule. If we don't, kids will only hear when they are breaking a rule or code of conduct. This can cause resentment, discouragement, less effort, or passive-aggressive behavior.

22. With Conscious Parenting, patience is mandatory. When you're not sure what to say or do—wait. And don't stress out trying to think of something to say. Trust that the optimal response will come to you at just the right time… and eventually, it will.

23. Many parents give their children positive feedback, then negative, then positive, then negative, and so on. The message is, "I like this behavior but not this one, and this one certainly displeases me."

This puts kids on the merry-go-round of seeking a parent's approval—a ride they feel they can never master (or ever could master). A misperception of conditional love can then set in. Conscious Parenting is the remedy to this situation.

24. Sometimes, a small positive behavior (or improvement) is hidden by a larger negative behavior. I call the positive behavior a SPARK. For example, a child may be slow to follow directions, but they don't argue like they have done in the past. Or a child may yell at a sibling, but they are not aggressive.

Focusing on the SPARK helps the positive behavior grow and the negative behavior to weaken. Overreacting to negative behavior often creates negative emotions in the parent and the child. All of this angry energy can actually strengthen the negative behavior the parent is trying to help their child change.

25. Don't just say, "Good job!" After a while, those words become meaningless. Instead, take the positive behavior you want to strengthen and "tie it together" with a word of praise: "I like how you are giving me good eye contact right now. You really seem to be tuning in."

26. One reason parents get so weary and burdened is that feelings accumulate, and unconscious interactions set in. Instead of really connecting and communicating with a child, parents react to unconscious mental projections and strong feelings about a child's past problems or some future concern.

Psych 101: The part of our nervous system that allows us to experience physical feelings also plays a part when we begin to talk about emotional feelings. The word emotion is derived from a French word meaning "agitate or stir up." So, a feeling is a disturbance of sorts. I am reminded of "Star Wars" when one of the Jedi Knights would get a serious expression and say, "I'm picking up a disturbance in the force." That's a good way to describe a feeling: it's a disturbance in our conscious awareness. From *Fingerpainting in Psych Class*, the chapter "Nothing More Than Feelings."

So, we can look at emotions (and thoughts to a lesser degree) as a disturbance in our conscious awareness. But if we turn inward and just notice the "disturbance," we begin to detach from it. If we can allow it to be there, all the thoughts and strong feelings can move through, and the disturbance will begin to subside.

27. Conscious Parenting is dealing with a child in the present moment. Parents do not allow feelings to accumulate, so interactions are always fresh and new.

28. If only we could acknowledge how far our child has come instead of going on and on about how far they have left to go.

Why not try this? At bedtime, give your child a positive summary of their day. See if you can fluidly discuss all of their positive or improved behavior for one minute or longer. You might have to prepare a little, but it's well worth it!

If you have been working with your child on their defiant behavior, point out and elaborate on times when they were a little more cooperative (or even a little less *un*cooperative). If you are working with them on better school behavior, be sure to comment on their perceived improvements—times when they were making more positive behavior choices—and fewer negative ones. If you are working with them on anger management, do the same: point out times when they were frustrated or mad but handled it better than in times past—they may have gotten angry, or they might have been loud, but they didn't threaten anyone, or become destructive, or aggressive. If you think about it, that's real progress!

When a child hears positive messages at bedtime, they are more likely to register and be received into a child's unconscious mind. These messages will make a much deeper impression than just talking to a child or lecturing them. And please don't muddy this exercise with any criticism or negativity.

Psych 101: Parents often wait for a child to manage their anger perfectly. Then we might notice the improvement (or we might not), and then we might give them a word of praise (or we might not). But then, for any small infraction—any sign of anger coming out in a way that signals ALERT!, we jump on them with both feet. This is a mistake. With anger management, no one can go from the first rung on the ladder to the very top. But, when we notice and comment on even small improvements, kids will keep climbing.

29. Conscious Parenting verbally connects a strategic compliment to a desirable behavior or improved attitude. This is very powerful in building a child up, coaxing them away from negative behavior, and strengthening the parent-child relationship.

30. The ultimate double bind: Unconscious behavior sucks, but we don't know it sucks because we're unconscious.

Why not try this? When we try not to think, pressure builds. Then, before we know it, thinking rushes back in and takes over again. Instead, try taking a short break from thinking. Try to walk to the kitchen without thinking. Try to climb some stairs without thinking. Try to wash your hands without thinking. Is thinking really required all the time? Even for these small things we've done a million times?

A small break from thinking can turn into a medium break and then a large break from thinking. Not thinking (called zen or non-conceptual awareness) puts us in the field of what Carl Jung called Universal Consciousness. Not thinking connects us to this field where we can experience ultimate peace, rediscover our higher self, and have access to uncommon knowledge and wisdom.

OCTOBER

1. Unconscious parenting can quickly lead to an antagonistic and adversarial relationship. Then, parents seem surprised that their child is not listening and working with them.

Conscious Parenting strategically builds and maintains a close, healthy relationship. Mutual respect and a high level of cooperation are the end result.

2. If we don't regularly have fun with our kids, they may begin to see us as "the warden" or "the cop on the beat." Then, working together is much less likely.

Have you laughed with your child today? If not, it may be time to have some fun. Adults can be so serious!

3.

 *The creative adult is the child who survived."*

— URSELA K. GUIN

Everyone has a child-like part to their personality. But we can't be Peter Pan. Much of our inner child succumbs to adulthood. But when we are children, harsh parenting and trauma also chip away at our inner child and does the most damage.

So, let's keep this in mind so we can parent with more sensitivity and not push our children to grow up so quickly. In return, maybe they can help us revive our inner child…

4.

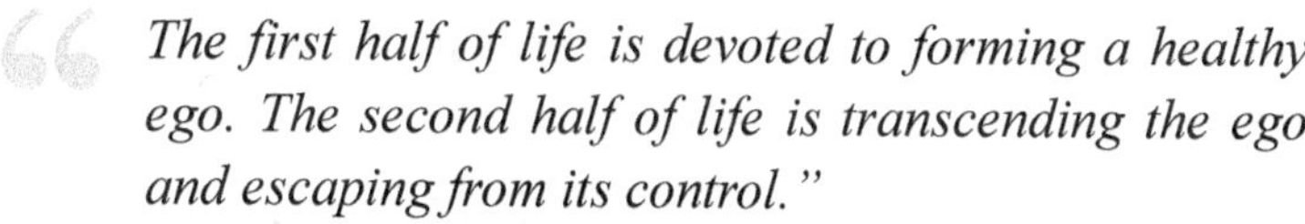

The first half of life is devoted to forming a healthy ego. The second half of life is transcending the ego and escaping from its control."

— ADAPTED FROM A QUOTE BY CARL JUNG

This quote reminds us that we have two choices: try to make our ego more healthy and somehow heal the unavoidable wounds we all suffer, or work to transcend the ego altogether.

5. If one parent reads to a child, the child will think that reading is important to that parent. If both parents read to a child, the child will likely think that reading is important.

Why not try this? Conscious Parenting Step-by-Step: To facilitate learning and get the best results, consider these steps:

- A parent teaches a child something new—not through a long narrative, but experientially. Positive feedback is given for effort and any forward movement. No extra directives are given, and critical statements are avoided.
- Provide a level of supervision that helps ensure a child succeeds in learning, practicing, and beginning to master their new skill. Provide plenty of positive feedback as a child takes steps toward practicing and learning the new behavior. Focus on an improvement over a previous try. If you criticize at this stage, a child might become frustrated, which can slow or disrupt the whole process.
- Check in periodically. Make sure a child continues to be successful and that the new skill is becoming, to some degree, habitual. No criticism is given.

Conscious parents should also consider the idea that maybe the child can improve upon the parent's method or that another method the child develops will be just as good or better—better because it is the child's idea, not the parent's.

6. Kids want to be noticed. They can get noticed in one of two ways: 1) reaching out for positive attention, or 2) they can reach out for some kind of negative attention. When children try to get positive attention, they put themselves out there emotionally. In this position, they are both open and vulnerable. If their attempt to get positive attention is ignored, or if they are mistreated ("How many times do I have to tell you to leave me alone when I get home from work?!?!"), it can be frustrating or painful for a child.

In contrast, negative attention is a slam dunk. These are behaviors that cannot be ignored. Kids will get noticed, and parental reactions are going to be very predictable—a parent will almost always give the child some form of negativity, either in words or in actions.

But why would a child choose negative attention? Because kids know that negative behavior cannot be ignored, so when they engage in negative behavior, THEY cannot be ignored. Some children can start to prefer this. They are then getting attention, albeit negative attention, on their own terms. They don't have to wait around in hopes that a parent will notice them being good.

Now the child feels powerful and in control, plus there is a mental buffer—a parent's negative reaction doesn't really hurt because the child sets up the negative situation in the first place. This egoic movement usually starts as a reflex and then turns into an unconscious way for a child to get their emotional needs met. But negative attention is no way to meet emotional needs. Parents must understand this process to bring a child back to getting their needs met in positive and healthy ways. (Note: Any negative attention stymies this process.) See *Fingerpainting in Psych Class* for more.

7. Relinquish control. You never had it, anyway.

You can manage, influence, persuade, affirm, nurture, love, and lots of other things, but control? No. Control is always an illusion. (Except for controlling yourself, of course. That's always doable.)

8. If a child is closed or angry, it is better to keep the peace than it is to make your point. You can make your point later after peace is restored.

Case Study: Sara, an eight-year-old patient, had learned to wash her hair, condition it, and rinse out all the shampoo and conditioner. Two months later, not shampooing and rinsing her hair fully had again become a problem. What happened?

Mom had taught Sara to wash and rinse her hair correctly. Then she supervised Sara's "washing her hair behavior" for a while, but backed off too quickly. Then Sarah regressed.

To remedy this, we went back to square one. We did a speedy review of the method. Mom supervised her and gave her lots of positive comments for "good, or improved, hair-washing behavior." Then, Mom spot-checked her in the shower, all the while keeping the positive comments coming. Sara got back up to speed in no time, finally internalizing this important daily living skill.

9. Before you say, "Well, let me tell you what I would do," ask your child questions and make comments to guide and help them arrive at their own special solution to a challenge they might be facing.

10. Until we stop taking our child's misbehavior personally—or see it as a reflection on us as a parent—we will be limited in how much we can help them and work with them effectively.

11. The first thing to do when you get angry is nothing; nothing until your anger passes; nothing until the good ideas return.

Anger management really should be called "anger *understanding* and management." In that way, people might stop trying to control their anger but instead try to understand it. And when they understand it, they will naturally be able to manage it better.

12. Ironically, the more we try to make a child happy, the more unhappy and discontent they can become. Happiness is and will continue to be an inside job. Teach and reinforce this truth early. Let's get off the tragic merry-go-round of trying to make kids happy.

13. Some parents believe that a child talking back is a challenge to their authority. And in a way, they're right.

A child talking back becomes a test for the parent. How will they exercise their authority at these times? Harshly and reactively? Or with patience and compassion?

Parents are the authority figures in the family, no matter how a child is acting. How we exercise that power is of the utmost importance to how a child matures, handles frustration, treats others, and how they relate to other authority figures.

14. A young child's only love language is a parent's attention. A parent's attention is like air to them. Let's give our children positive attention so they will feel no need to try to get our negative attention.

15. If we try to bend a child's will with power and authority, we might weaken the bond and damage the relationship. If we try to perfect our ability to relate felt love, a child will be more likely to follow our lead.

Psych 101: Passive-aggressive behaviors are unconscious, indirect displays of anger toward another. They can be words or actions. Passive-aggressive behavior reactively "leaks out of us" until we go through the forgiveness process. Until then, we are bound to the other person by the pain they have caused us…

16.

> *When another person makes us suffer, it is because they suffer deeply within themself, and their suffering is spilling over. They do not need punishment; they need help.*

— THICH NHAT HANH

17. "Ahhh! It's not working! All these affirming comments, shaping positive behavior and conveying love, and there's no change in my child's behavior! I'm listening. I'm involved. I'm warm and affectionate. What am I doing wrong?"

Well, sometimes nothing. There is a certain amount of lag time with Conscious Parenting. We have to be in this for the long haul. We definitely can't afford to drift back and forth between conscious and unconscious parenting, revisiting the "old ways" when things get difficult or too heated. We have to stay the course with a steely resolve. We trust and have faith that Conscious Parenting will melt away problem behaviors and turn a wayward child around.

18. If our mood and behavior are erratic, there is a high probability that our child's mood and behavior will be erratic, too. Let's find our calm center first before we speak or act.

19. If we fail to acknowledge a child's small attempts at being responsible, they might become discouraged and lapse into less responsible or more irresponsible behavior.

20. Some people try not to get angry and deny or suppress angry feelings, while some people reactively blast others when they are angry.

Anger management is always a balancing act. The balance is being honest with our angry feelings while not fueling them with angry self-talk. We must also be open so anger can pass. Then, we take the time to formulate a conscious response where our thoughts and feelings are shared but in a compassionate manner. With practice, this method becomes the norm.

21. When we sacrifice our relationship to try to stay in control of our child, we may well lose both.

22. Many times, a child will stop some negative behavior on their own. Then, a parent has a great opportunity to say, "I'm impressed. Right now, you just told yourself to stop (whatever they were doing), and I didn't even have to say anything. How very grown up of you!"

Why not try this? Many behavior problems can be avoided altogether."You guys are getting along!" will help keep an argument from ever arising, or "I like how you are staying so close to me!" will help keep a child from wandering too far away from Mom or Dad when they are out. Be proactive. Notice naturally occurring positive behavior and make it the focus of your attention.

23. The best way to raise a responsible child is to focus on and point out all of their responsible (or more responsible) behavior, not to go on and on about all the ways they are still irresponsible.

24. Consistently show your child love, and when they grow up, they will have an ample supply of love for themself and others.

25. Your child is a very important part of the family—an integral part of the family. However, a child should not be the center of the family. That's too much on them. Parents who center everything around their kids lose their balance and their effectiveness. The parent-child relationship will likely suffer or not be as healthy as it could be. Love your children. Meet their needs. But don't make a child the center of all your time and attention.

26. Lasting change will always start with the one, not the many. And real change will always be an inside job, not just changing outer behavior.

27. We will stop pushing our children so much when we remember what it was like to be pushed.

Why not try this? "Right now, you are using your purple crayon and drawing circles at the bottom of your paper."

"Your brother said something really mean, and now you look angry."

"You have four dolls sitting together in a row. Now you're getting out your tea set. Is someone having a tea party?"

These are examples of active recognition. A compliment says, "I'm happy with your behavior!" and criticism says, "I'm not happy with your behavior!" But active recognition says, "I am interested in you and what you're doing."

With active recognition, there is no judgment on whether a behavior is good or bad, and therein lies its power.

28. A child will raise their voice and be disrespectful. That's because kids have strong feelings and haven't learned how to manage them yet.

And kids can be egocentric and selfish. They say and do things without adequate empathy.

And, kids want what they want, not what we want for them—and they don't mind battling to get their way, no matter who they might hurt.

Plus, kids don't understand how yelling and disrespect damage relationships.

But as adults? As adults, we have to do better.

29. Love is gentle… even when it has to be tough.

30. A parent can convey love all day long, but one act of harsh insensitivity might bring that love into question…

31. Don't let worry and anxiety over a child's behavior turn into anger and scorn. Relate your concern—set parameters. Enforce them. Build insight. Resist the urge to control. And most importantly, enthusiastically comment on improved behavior or periods when negative behavior is not present.

NOVEMBER

1.

To a child, 'love' is spelled 'T-I-M-E.'"

— ZIG ZIGLER

Time with your child. *Quality time* with your child. Make it your conscious intent…

2.

It's what we think we know that keeps us from learning."

— CLAUDE BERNARD

Sometimes, our old hand-me-down beliefs keep us from being open to new information that may be more accurate and useful.

3.

As a parent, the coolest tool I learned was when one of my kids was upset or started complaining about something; I would say, 'Do you need me to get involved, offer advice, or just listen to you'?"

— TOBIAS S. BUCKELL

4. Graciousness and civility will often be mistaken for weakness and naivety, usually by weak or naive people.

5. Some kids might not change because their parents work too hard to change them.

6. Until you are able to observe an angry reaction, you are at the mercy of it.

7. Parents are always leading by example… whether they know it or not.

Why not try this? Many, if not most of us, think critically. We mistakenly believe this is normal.

It is hard for a child to notice when they're thinking critically. The younger the child, the more difficult it is. For this reason, I developed the Five Words activity.

The Five Words are, in this order

- like,
- love,
- good,
- great,
- thank you.

With "thank you," similar words can be included, like "grateful" or "appreciate"—any word that shows gratitude.

First, have a child memorize the five words in order. Then, the facilitator uses the word "like" in a sentence. Example: "I like Cheerios." Then, it's the child's turn to use the word "love" in a sentence. It's back-and-forth like this until all five words are used. (To simplify, everyone can use the word "like," then "love," and so on.)

The Five Words can also be a wonderful group or family activity. Do the exercise in a way where each person gets a different word on each round. I don't know how many times I have seen this little exercise change the energy or mood in an individual or a family. If one child refuses to play, play anyway. They will still benefit by being close and hearing everyone's responses. Positivity is like that...

Over time, participants will branch out, using more and more positive words, while all the negative words begin to fade into the background. Remember: When we change our speech, our thoughts must change as well.

8. We cannot really connect with a child unless we play with them and talk to them about things in which they are interested. These become positive connection points—ways to convey love, stay close, and help a child build a positive self-image.

Why not try this? Instead of wading into a lecture or giving a reprimand, why not say to your child, "Can I talk to you about something?" or, "May I suggest something?" If a child says 'yes,' then proceed. If a child says 'no,' then set up a time when you both can talk. Being more respectful of your child usually results in more openness from your child.

Psych 101: The three soils parable: In the parenting business, we will do best if we keep this parable in mind. It is found in the New Testament.

A farmer was planting his field. Some seeds fell on shallow soil. Here, the seeds quickly grew but never developed a strong root system, so the sun burned them up.

Other seeds fell on rocky soil. These seeds were quickly eaten by hungry birds.

But most of the seeds fell into the deep, rich soil. These seeds developed a strong root system and grew to their full capacity.

The moral of the story is that parents should learn to wait until their child is showing openness and interest. Good soil only. Let's not waste our breath on shallow or rocky soil.

9. One of the quickest ways to become angry is to unconsciously expect our child or partner to behave like we would.

10. One of the most unconscious things we do is wait for someone else to change before we do the work we need to do.

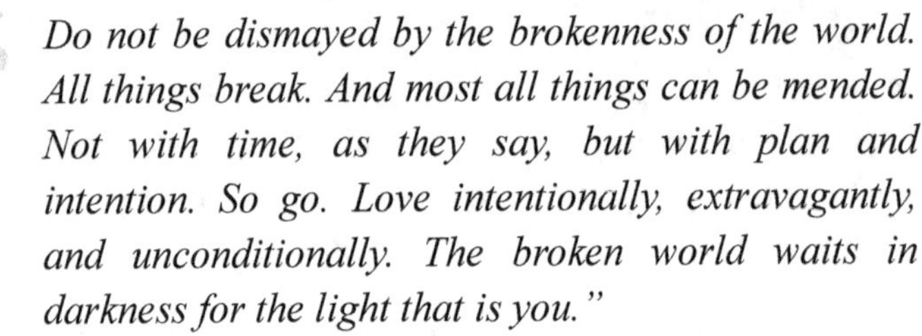

> *Do not be dismayed by the brokenness of the world. All things break. And most all things can be mended. Not with time, as they say, but with plan and intention. So go. Love intentionally, extravagantly, and unconditionally. The broken world waits in darkness for the light that is you."*

— ADAPTED FROM A QUOTE BY L. R. KNOST

11. Don't just talk to your child about self-restraint. Let them see and experience it in you.

12. If we said, "I hate somebody," and the person we "hate" became physically injured or sick, would we continue to so recklessly use that word?

If we said, "I hate… (some situation)," and the situation we "hate" became even worse, and more bad situations followed, would we continue to so recklessly use that word?

And, if we said, "I hate something," and the thing we "hate" began to expand until we were being crushed by it, would we continue to so recklessly use that word? Life is hard, and people will hurt us, but nothing and no one can make us hate.

13. Before you tell a child how they might do something quicker or better, give pause. They are learning something for themself.

14. Anticipate good behavior. Notice good behavior. Affirm good behavior. Does this guarantee good behavior? No. But it's as close as we will get.

Case Study: I walked into a classroom to check on a client. I didn't know it, but 6-year-old Nicholas was in timeout. He must have seen a chance to escape because out into the hallway, he gleefully ran (this is strong evidence of negative attention-seeking. Nicholas seemed to be enjoying the negative drama he was creating in the classroom). Feeling at least partly responsible, I went after him. The teacher looked relieved.

Before he got too far ahead of me, I called after him, "Are we going on an adventure?" (This was my playful and immediate attempt to connect with Nicholas.)

Nicholas slowed a little, probably curious because I didn't say, "Nicholas! Get back here!" I made eye contact and pointed. "That way could be interesting, but I don't know. I wouldn't mind seeing what's down that way, too. What do you think?" (I engaged Nicholas in a light-hearted way. There was no pressure or rushing. This was another attempt to connect with him.)

He gave me a once-over look as if he was sizing me up. He pointed to his left and started walking while I fell in behind him. (I tried to make Nicholas feel important, and I again tried to connect with him.)

In a short time, Nicholas and I started talking. I brought the discussion back to his time out.

"So what happened?" I asked Nicholas.

"I wouldn't do my work," he said.

"Was it hard?" I asked.

"No. It's easy, just boring." Nicholas rolled his eyes.

What are you going to do next?" I asked.

He paused. "I don't know. I guess I should go back. Maybe I should do some work."

"What a good idea! Do you need help?" I asked.

"No, I'm good," he said.

And he was, too…

Remember. Conscious Parenting is working *with* kids, not *on* them.

15. Mental preoccupation and Conscious Parenting don't mix. Be here—with your child—now.

16. Don't let obtaining more data be more important than applying the Conscious Parenting information you already possess.

17. "Mom, thanks for coming behind me to make sure I do everything right!" said no kid ever.

Why not try this?

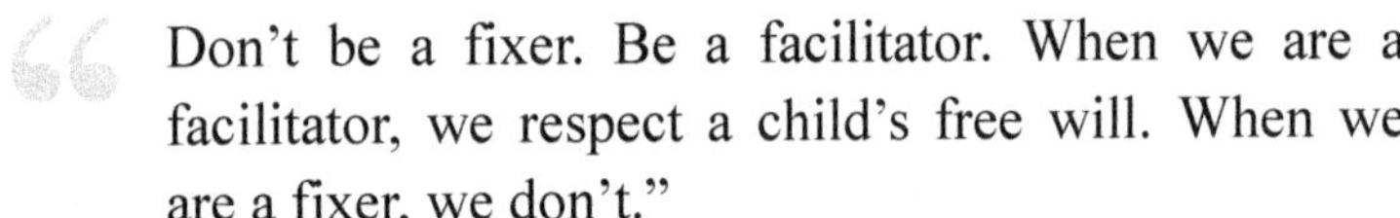

> Don't be a fixer. Be a facilitator. When we are a facilitator, we respect a child's free will. When we are a fixer, we don't."

— JAY MORGAN

When we fail to respect a child's free will, we will unconsciously try to control them (or a situation). When kids sense they are trying to be controlled, many will rebel. So, trying to control our kids moves us further away from achieving what we really want for them, whatever that might be. While facilitating is tricky and more difficult, it works better because a child's free will is always acknowledged and honored.

18. When our child overreacts, and we don't overreact back, we show them the possibility of self-control and self-discipline. When our child says something mean-spirited, and we don't say anything mean back, we show them the possibility of compassion and unconditional love.

Why not try this? I have seen many kids beg their parents for a pet. When they wear their parents down and finally get a puppy, the child often doesn't take care of it. Sometimes, they are even mean to their pet—the one they felt like they just couldn't live without. This situation creates strife in the household—and usually extra work for the parents.

Children do benefit greatly when they learn to take care of things. It pulls them out of themselves. It helps them discover what an outward mindset is like.

So, if a child wants a pet, give them a plant. Choose a plant that is easy to care for. Then it's up to them to not only keep it alive but to make it thrive. Next, you might get a trickier plant, one that will require more of a child's attention. And, if they're again successful, it may be time for a goldfish or a turtle.

Note: If your child gets angry and is non-acceptant, please don't get them anything.

Remind yourself that you are not being mean—you are waiting for your child. They are choosing not to work within the parameters that you, a loving parent, have set for them.

19.

We don't stop playing because we grow old. We grow old because we stop playing."

— GEORGE BERNARD SHAW

20. It is much better to praise a child for their hard work and persistence, not just for their successes. Then, they will be more likely to become a hard worker with persistence—not an adult who chases the next success and become devastated when they fail.

21. Bringing up a child's past mistakes has no therapeutic value. On the contrary, it sows seeds of self-doubt in some children and resentment in others.

22. A peaceful home is a gift we give to our children—a tricky, complicated, difficult, but very precious gift. With this upbringing, an imprint is made. Then, when a child is older, they will seek out the familiar, the same thing, a peaceful coexistence with others. In this way, a parent's inner peace becomes, or at the very least contributes to, a family's peace. This is true community.

23. When our inner peace is greater than the outer drama, we are free to act consciously with volition and are no longer a part of the outer drama.

24. When you are in tune with your child, it makes for a truly beautiful melody.

25.

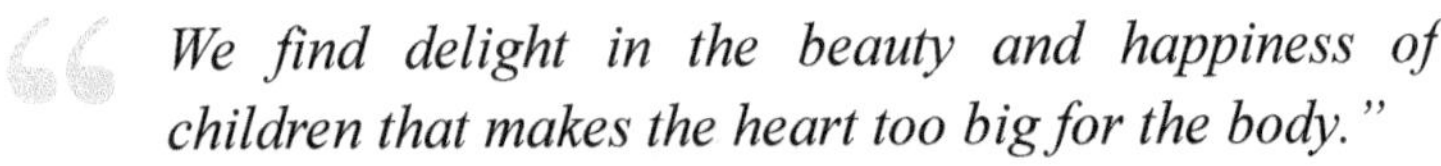

We find delight in the beauty and happiness of children that makes the heart too big for the body."

— RALPH WALDO EMERSON

Let's see if we can discover or rediscover this perspective. Let's see if we can look at our child in this way at least one time a day. (Two times if you want to be an overachiever.)

Psych 101: Carl Jung said, "There is no coming to consciousness without pain." Over 2,000 years earlier, the Buddha said, "Suffering is the greatest teacher." What?!?!

In Buddhism, *The First Noble Truth* states that "Life is suffering." Scott Peck, in his groundbreaking book *The Road Less Traveled*, toned things down for his predominantly Western audience by writing, "Life is difficult." Is it possible that life is designed to be difficult—that life is supposed to cause us pain and suffering?

In the beloved story, *Peter Pan*, the main character, Peter, never grew up. Instead, he chose frivolousness and continuous play. Peter also fled from uncomfortable situations and feelings, sending Wendy packing when their "pretend relationship" began to turn into a real one—one with deep and, at times, conflicted feelings. Peter's avoidance and escapism resulted in him staying a child. (Note: Peter was abandoned by his parents. Fairies found him and took him to Neverland. There the continual distraction and play helped Peter avoid dealing with the pain from his abandonment. While Peter became fun-loving and carefree, he also became avoidant, boastful, and self-centered.)

There seems to be a Peter Pan in all of us. Freud called this part of our psyche the Id. Like Peter, the Id doesn't want to grow up either. (Hint: This is where pain and suffering come in…)

As difficult as it is to accept, people seem to need pain and suffering to grow. If we are really in a jam or feeling miserable—and we don't give ourselves over to hopelessness—we are often highly motivated to get out of the bad situation, feel better, and try to improve ourselves. The pain and suffering shake us out of our complacency so we are willing to consider new ideas that before we wouldn't have given a moment's notice.

Scott Peck went on to write a perplexing and thought-provoking passage. Peck wrote, "Once we truly know that life is difficult—once we truly understand and accept it—then life is no longer difficult. Because once it is accepted, the fact that life is difficult no longer matters."

It took me a while to even begin to glean the meaning of this passage, but in everyday speech, here's what I think Peck was saying: When we have deeply convinced ourselves that *life is difficult* (and it's supposed to be); and that unavoidable pain will come our way, then, when life is difficult and when pain comes our way, we are no longer surprised. We can allow the pain to be there, no longer resist it, and feel it fully. Then as our feelings neutralize, we become solution-focused. We begin to formulate a conscious response to the situation at hand. This response requires no negative thinking, no ruminating, and no feeling sorry for ourselves. We get out of negative thinking mode and into productive thinking mode, where a solution can be found.

Remember, thinking creates most of our pain and suffering, so this one step keeps us from making the inevitable pain and suffering any worse.

Silver lining: Life is a reflection of our thinking and our attitude. When we detach from old, conditioned, negative thinking and the voice in our head fades, our mind becomes fertile ground for dream realization.

26. Remember: Children are blessings—even if they aren't behaving particularly well.

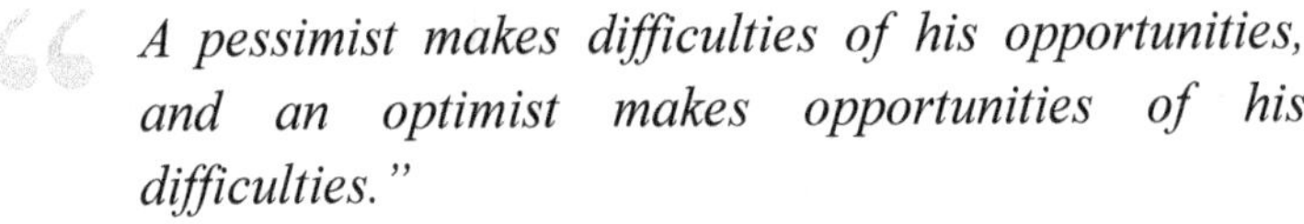

> *A pessimist makes difficulties of his opportunities, and an optimist makes opportunities of his difficulties."*

> — HARRY S. TRUMAN

27. Harshness and scare tactics result in fearfully compliant kids or angry semi-compliant ones.

28. They say love will find a way. I prefer "Love will *lead* the way."

29. If real estate is "Location. Location. Location." Then Conscious Parenting is "Relationship. Relationship. Relationship."

30. Negative behavior screams at you, while positive behavior whispers. Listen for the whispers. Try not to miss them. Otherwise, we will be energizing our child's loud, harsh, or negative behavior.

1. When children mess up, they need our help and guidance, not just consequences and punishment.

Psych 101: Some specialists in the field have suggested that effective parenting involves finding the balance between love and discipline. They say that, on the one hand, a parent must demonstrate and convey love, but on the other hand, a parent must discipline a child when needed. While 1 basically agree with this model, I do see a potential problem: The love, on the one hand, is entirely too far from discipline on the other.

In actuality, discipline—a part of which is imposing consequences—is an extension and a special expression of a parent's love for a child. It is confusing and potentially damaging to view love and discipline as somehow separate. From *Fingerpainting in Psych Class*.

2. Strong emotional reactions are a display of one's outer power. Conscious responses are an exercise and display of one's inner power.

3. Troubles and problems are growth opportunities… in disguise.

> *A person cannot truly solve a problem at the same level of consciousness where the problem was created."*

— ADAPTED FROM A QUOTE BY ALBERT EINSTEIN

4.

   Our thoughts are only suggestions on what to say and
do, not mandates."

5.

"What is love? asked the student.

"The total absence of fear," said the master.

"What is it we fear?" asked the student.

"Love," said the master.

–ANTHONY DE MELLO

6. Instead of trying to win or be the best, let's teach our kids to try
to do better, learning to focus on their own small improvements.

In any competition, a balance can be achieved. A child plays to
win, but they also play to have fun. Then, if they don't win, at least
they had a good time and probably improved their skill level.
Competition unnecessarily creates one winner and many losers.

7. Kids follow the energy. Let's make sure our child's positive
behavior gets our energy—not their negative.

Case Study: A dad told his 12-year-old daughter, Bella, to go
clean her room. Bella rolled her eyes and mumbled something
disrespectful as she slowly plodded to her room. Every fiber of
Dad's being wanted to say, "Just lose the attitude, Bella, and do
what I said!"

But fortunately, he didn't. Instead, he called her back. Bella turned
toward him angrily, bracing for a fight. Her whole demeanor said,
"Now what?!?!"

Dad devised a reframe. He looked at Bella calmly and said, "Bella, I'm proud of you. You don't like to clean your room, and it's a real mess, but right away you started walking to your room to clean it. You don't want to clean it, but it looks like you're going to clean it anyway. That's great! Making ourselves do things we don't want to do is a critical life skill. You're building inner strength—strength you will need to tackle other tough or undesirable tasks now and as you get older." Bella's attitude softened. She went to her room and did a great job.

(A reframe is describing a child's negative behavior in a positive way or in a way that suggests an improvement over a similar behavior from the past).

8. You can be as gentle as you want until your child's behavior demands that you be firm. But can we be firm without lapsing into trying to control?

9.

A child is not an empty vessel to be filled, but a lamp to be lit."

— ROBERT H. SHAFFER

10. Where listening is undervalued, talking will be overutilized. If a parent isn't sure what to say or do, they can always go back to active listening and reflection.

11. The more conscious we become, the more hesitant we will be to criticize anyone and the more generous we will be with our praise and appreciation.

Psych 101: It was Nolan's turn to teach me something important…

Nolan is a 14-year-old who has autism. He has a lot of social anxiety, and some of his teachers give him a hard time. And sometimes, his peers, who do not understand him, make mean and insensitive remarks. Nolan has superior intelligence but has grown to hate school. The night before a school day, he begins to panic. He starts to worry and obsess over the negative aspects of school and the bad things that have happened to him there.

In one session, I presented an important principle: *if we change our speech, our thoughts have to change, too.* I challenged him to start naming things about school that he liked. Nolan had a very difficult time naming anything. Finally, he said, "Can I just name the things that are tolerable?"

I said, "Absolutely!" So, he started carefully naming things that he could tolerate or put up with. What a wonderful reminder that:

- Kids can often come up with solutions that are perfectly fine, or even better than the ones we could devise, and
- Kids go at their own pace, not ours.

12. It's amazing how well most kids do when we stop talking about their failures and start talking about their successes.

13. Conscious Parenting is ego-less parenting. As a parent notices how their ego works—how it tries to strengthen or add to itself, or how it tries to defend itself from a perceived attack—they begin to pull away from egoic influence.

With less ego, kids have less to push against. Then, they will likely be more open and cooperative.

Within the ego, there is no lasting peace. That's because the ego is always in a state of wanting or in defense mode because the ego realizes its own impermanence. But the higher self has none of these limitations.

14. A gentle approach to life (and parenting) tends to result in a gentle response *from* Life—and from our children.

Case Study: I once worked with a delightful 15-year-old named Amber. She presented with generalized anxiety and panic, which was particularly bad when she was around a large group of people.

I first helped Amber understand how anxiety worked. Together, we identified some of her "anxious thought loops" (old anxious thinking patterns), which she learned generated most of her anxiety. These feelings then accumulated in her psyche (or her inner self), causing her anxious symptoms. Amber then practiced conscious breathing techniques to counteract her shallow, anxious breathing, plus she learned simple meditation, which helped her notice her anxious thoughts so she was not so affected by them. Not surprisingly, Amber's anxiety began to diminish.

In one session, Amber shared what she had learned about her perfectionistic thinking. As she was meditating, Amber clearly noticed an inner voice that told her that she wasn't "good enough," "smart enough," "attractive enough," and so on. Amber now realized this was an old way of thinking from an earlier time in her life when she was more anxious and unsure of herself. With this insight, these thoughts didn't bother Amber nearly as much.

Amber began to notice even more anxious thinking. One thought tried to convince her that she would never master the algebra she had just learned in class. Amber noticed this thought from outside her thinking mind and decided that she would change it a little and add the word "yet."

Now, Amber did not have to settle for the unsettling thought, "I'll never figure out these equations!" Instead, she modified it to, "I haven't figured out these equations... *yet.*" This new thought was conscious and open-ended, not a negative self-assessment written in stone. The meaning that Amber created was, "I don't understand the math yet, but you can bet I will!"

(Note: In psychology, this is called cognitive restructuring.)

15. When we address our child's behavior problems positively and encouragingly, a child will grow up and be more likely to address their life challenges positively and encouragingly, too.

16. If a person is quick to anger, they should be slow to speak and act.

The Buddha said that anger is like "a plant with a honeyed tip and a poisoned root."

Some people seem to regularly need angry energy to make them feel complete (to make their ego feel complete). These people seem to relish the idea of "letting somebody have it!" or "putting someone in their place!" or "telling someone how it really is!" For them, this is the "honeyed tip" of which the Buddha spoke. At an unconscious level, the angry energy they generate seems irresistible, although they would probably be the last ones to agree with this interpretation. An angry exchange can make an angry person feel powerful and satisfied. They can even convince themself they engaged in an honorable act.

But all of the angry person's words and actions come from a "poisoned root." So all of their words and the energy behind their words become poison to the giver and poison to the receiver.

Why not try this? Invent a game with your child using household items and random toys. Let your child lead the activity as much as they are able. Connecting with a child through fun and creativity? *Priceless…*

17. A family is a group of people who use their love to create something much bigger—Family love.

18. Don't fool yourself into believing that talking more loudly to your child will increase the likelihood they will hear you, listen to you, and seriously consider what you are trying to say.

19.

> *The illiterate of the 21st century will not be those who cannot read and write but those who cannot learn, unlearn, and relearn.*"

— ALVIN TOFFLER

20. Count your blessings—all of the things you have to be thankful for—today and every day.

Living a life of gratitude makes the stressful and unpleasant things in life begin to melt away…

Why not try this? Let kids fail…

What?!?! That sounds ridiculous, maybe even dangerous. Or does it?

When my kids were young, I felt a strong urge to teach them the right way to do things (in retrospect, this was more like *my way of doing things*). But then it finally hit me—I was keeping them from learning! The way they wanted to fold the towels, organize their toys, or do their homework may not have been the way I would've done it, but it often worked. Then, when it didn't work, I didn't need to say much. They were already moving on to Plan B. And if they got frustrated, a few encouraging words were all they needed to try again.

If you want your child to be successful, don't deny them these small learning opportunities and the small, medium and sometimes large failures that will come their way. Kids will be more successful when we give them space to learn, space to practice, space to succeed, and, yes, even space to fail.

21. Be proactive. Focus on positive behavior, and amazingly, negative behavior will lessen, often without a need for consequences or punishment. Plus, your positive messages become building blocks that a child will use to build a more positive self-image. Don't pollute this wonderful process with criticism and discouraging remarks.

22. When we drop our mental expectations, we're free to accept another person fully and to love them unconditionally. We are then giving that person our complete permission to be themself.

23. The price we must pay for true love is our ego.

24. Let the seasonal lights remind you of your own inner light. Wishing you a happy and conscious holiday season!

Allowing a child the freedom to be themself is the most extraordinary gift a parent can give.

25.

> *Opinion is really the lowest form of human knowledge. It requires no accountability and no understanding. The highest form of knowledge is empathy, for it requires us to suspend our egos so we can live in another's world."*

> — BILL BULLARD

(Note: Practicing empathy weakens the ego and helps us sense our connectedness to all that is.)

Why not try this? Lots of children are "revved up." They never seem to slow down. Being still for some children seems to be a monumental task.

There are lots of different reasons for kids being revved up, but the cure for each case is the same: begin stillness training.

Get out a calendar. Tell your child you're going to time them on how long they can be perfectly still and quiet, like a statue. Get a stop watch and try to make quiet training very official-looking. For younger children, special allowances must be made, but as they get older, parents raise their expectations.

With stillness training, kids can easily break their records. This makes them feel good. What are they feeling good about? Being still and quiet.

Keep track of your child's high score record, but also keep track of their longest days-in-a-row record. For instance, if a child earned scores of three minutes, three minutes and 10 seconds, and then went down to one and a half minutes, they may feel discouraged. But when you look at the statistics, you can make them aware that their high score record was three minutes and 10 seconds, but they also have three days in a row with stillness training scores of at least one and 1/2 minutes, and that's a new personal best record! Always present the data in the most encouraging way possible.

 *Being still becomes a bridge to calmness."*

— JAY MORGAN

No one can discover calmness until they can be still. As we are physically still, our body naturally relaxes. Watch your child doing stillness training, and somewhere between three and five minutes, they will probably let out a sigh. They are beginning to decompress and calm down.

During stillness training, our thoughts may initially rev up, but then they will begin to slow down. Being still allows our body to naturally guide us back into, not only calmness but a relaxed state, and, as we continue our practice, peacefulness. Our thinking mind doesn't have a clue.

26. The happier (content + peaceful) we are with ourselves, the more happiness we bring to our relationships, and the less dependent we are on needing other people to make us happy. Then, we are free to enjoy each other—no strings attached.

27. Taking complete responsibility for our happiness is a game (and life) changer!

28. When kids feel appreciated, they tend to cooperate and do more than what is expected.

Let's be sure to notice and verbally appreciate all of our child's efforts.

29. If we can get in the habit of pausing before we say or do something, taking a conscious breath, reconnecting with our body, going to one of our five senses, or reminding ourselves of what our child means to us, it becomes impossible to behave unconsciously.

30. Children will have to overcome many things. One of them should not be a parent's discouragement and negativity.

31. Every plant matures and blooms in its own time.

As a parent, work with your child. Help them when they need help.

But periodically remind yourself that this beautiful, one-of-a-kind little person in front of you—the one you have the privilege of tending to for only a short time—is growing and maturing and will bloom in their own time.

If you found this book helpful, help someone else! Go back to the website where you purchased *The Conscious Parenting Handbook* and enter a review.

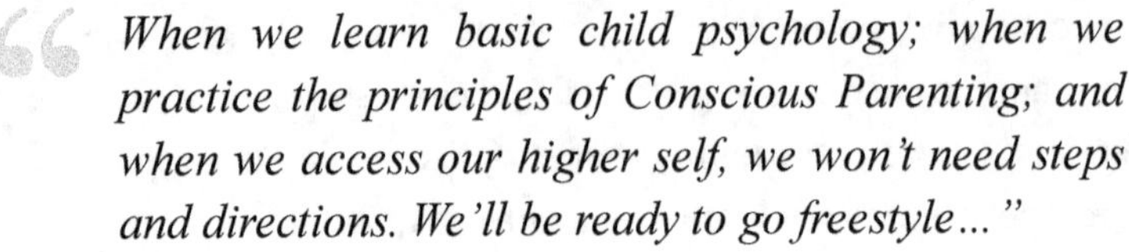

When we learn basic child psychology; when we practice the principles of Conscious Parenting; and when we access our higher self, we won't need steps and directions. We'll be ready to go freestyle..."

— JAY MORGAN

APPENDIX A

Conscious Parenting Affirmations

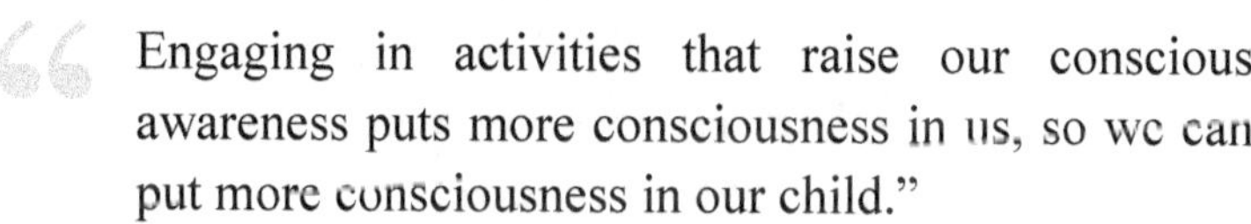

Engaging in activities that raise our conscious awareness puts more consciousness in us, so we can put more consciousness in our child."

— *THE CONSCIOUS PARENTING HANDBOOK,*
MARCH 21ST

You're still reading. I love it!

I bet you've learned a lot about Conscious Parenting. And I hope you already see improvements. But sometimes "head knowledge" is not enough. We often need practical application to make it stick —something experiential to bring it alive.

Welcome to The Conscious Parenting Affirmations Page!

One of the best ways to take our Conscious Parenting to the next level is to use positive affirmations. With a positive affirmation, we work on one thing at a time for a certain period of time—in this case, one week.

This section contains two sets of **52 positive affirmations**—That's one Conscious Parenting affirmation for each week of the year... times two!

With an affirmation, we are not just changing a behavior; we are changing the thoughts and disconnecting the impulses that *unconsciously create that behavior.* Awesome, right? But what if we went one step further? What if we took a positive affirmation and *combined it with some Conscious Parenting posts?*

In the next section, you will find all *The Conscious Parenting Handbook* posts listed by category. Now you can read and meditate on your weekly affirmation, but at the same time, reread posts from *The Handbook* which have a similar theme. This will provide the reader with a much wider and deeper perspective and help merge knowledge and application. Consistently working these affirmations, while reading related posts, will quickly help any parent be more conscious with their children.

But we must remember that unconscious parenting is formidable; it has a deep hold on us. Devoting ourselves to activities that raise our conscious awareness loosens that hold so we can become the Conscious Parent, and person, we always wanted to be (*and were meant to be*).

This process is not easy. The path of Conscious Parenting meanders and often gets bumpy. Many times, unconsciousness will rush back in and take us over. Sometimes our attempts at being conscious will blow up in our face. And other times we might get horribly discouraged and begin to think that we'll never get it right...

Note: As a rule, before any significant awakening, there's a "dark night of the soul." I see this as the ego's last, desperate attempt to keep a person ego-bound and to prevent them from realizing any real change and spiritual growth. So, when we are in this dark place, let's be sure to remind ourselves that we must be close to a breakthrough! Then we can become still... and silently watch for the thoughts that torment us. This simple process helps us detach from egoic thought—the sick thinking that generates most of our emotional pain.

My advice? When things are going well— but especially when they are not—pick up *The Handbook*. Casually read through the entries. Reread and meditate on those posts that are particularly relevant and meaningful. You might even want to purchase the audiobook. Continuously hearing and processing Conscious information is powerful and can really make the difference. For me, I repeatedly listened to three Eckhart Tolle cassette tapes on my commute to and from work. I listened to them every day for months until I had memorized them. When we listen to something that contains wisdom and truth, it disrupts and cuts through shallow egoic thinking. I believe this was a primary factor that led to my own spiritual awakening.

Regularly taking in conscious information and regularly taking advantage of opportunities to create pure awareness ensures our success. **Just don't give up**. Remember, Consciousness will always win, one way or another!

SELF-AFFIRMATIONS WITH ASSOCIATED POSTS

1. "I can choose to show love, no matter how I feel."
2. "My love is powerful."
3. "I choose positivity."
4. "My love is gentle and strong."
5. "I will infuse my child with the love I feel for them."
6. "I will be calm so I can help my child learn to be calm too."
7. "I believe in positive parenting."

8. "I will try not to get in a hurry… with anything."
9. "My strong-willed child is gifted in a special way. They are not a burden."
10. "I will notice my child's positive behavior, not just their negative behavior."
11. "I will almost always do best when I consciously do one thing at a time."
12. "I will tell my child 'Thank you' when they engage in a behavior I want to strengthen."
13. "I am the boss (or leader) in the family, not my child."
14. "My family is a team. We will work together."
15. "I will look for ways to build a cooperative spirit."
16. "I will find balance in my life."
17. "I will make my home a place of learning."
18. "I am ultimately responsible for educating myself and my child."
19. "I will try to understand first, not punish."
20. "I am improving my listening skills every day."
21. "I am more in charge of myself, so I am more in charge of the situation."
22. "I will listen to understand—not to respond."
23. "I will allow my breath to keep me centered and grounded."
24. "I will create a pause to help me not overreact."
25. "I will calmly discuss things."
26. "I will remember the seven words and use them whenever needed: I'm- Not- Going- to- Argue- With- You."
27. "I will carefully consider my words before I speak."
28. "I am a patient person."
29. "I will not give ultimatums. I will start with a polite request."
30. "I am a peaceful parent."
31. "I trust in the power of love."

32. "I will remember that harshness hurts my credibility as a parent."
33. "I will learn about and try to use detachment."
34. "I will let Conscious Parenting transform me."
35. "I will use Conscious Parenting to help my child build better behavior."
36. "My relationship with my child is more important than their behavior."
37. "I see the positive in my child."
38. "I am a Conscious Parent."
39. "I am a force for good in my child's life."
40. "I will not allow a disagreement to harm my relationship with my child."
41. "I will be emotionally available."
42. "I will work to understand my child's thinking and perspective without interjecting mine."
43. "I will avoid power struggles with my child."
44. "I will be mindful of how I connect with my child."
45. "I will teach my child self-love, so they won't get stuck in self-esteem."
46. "I will gently guide my child without trying to control them."
47. "I will show appreciation for all my child's efforts."
48. "I am conscious and aware."
49. "I will regularly take breaks from thinking throughout the day so I can practice pure awareness."
50. "I am calm and self-controlled."
51. "I will train myself to notice my child's positive behavior and improvements."
52. "My best decisions will always come from my inner calmness."

Work your positive affirmation for one week, and then move on to the next. But who likes the same thing over and over again? So, here are 52 more positive affirmations, one for every week of *another* year.

CONSCIOUS PARENTING AFFIRMATIONS:

Think them… Work them… Then watch the magic…

1. "I have confidence in my child and their abilities."
2. "I will be an encourager."
3. "When my child thinks different than me, I will try to understand, not freak out."
4. "I respect my child's free will even when they are not cooperative."
5. "I will be gentle with myself so I can be gentle with my child."
6. "I will be positive and encouraging so my child will be open and more likely to listen to me."
7. "I will not engage in scolding."
8. "I will remember that loving actions are more powerful than loving words."
9. "Outer drama is no match for my inner peace."
10. "I choose love."
11. "I will control my words and actions."
12. "I am growing in my ability to be a conscious parent."
13. "I will practice intentional parenting."
14. "I will always try to 'be… here… now.'"
15. "Being positive is one way I show love."
16. "I choose to be positive."
17. "I can't afford to just act calm. I must be calm."
18. "I am a conscious influencer."
19. "I will unplug and do something every day to be a calmer person."
20. "I choose self-compassion and gently embrace and affirm myself."

21. "I do not have to have the last word."
22. "I will notice and comment on what's going right so I can keep things from going wrong."
23. "I choose positive parenting."
24. "I will not underestimate the power of kindness."
25. "With Conscious Parenting, I can forgive myself and start over at any time."
26. "Being critical and harsh is not for me."
27. "I choose peace, not drama."
28. "I will lead by example."
29. "I will touch my child's life today in the best possible way."
30. "I believe in open communication with no interrupting."
31. "I will seek out quietness several times a day, even if it's only for one minute."
32. "I will hug my children often."
33. "I will voice appreciation for my child's positive behavior."
34. "I will be kind because my child deserves kindness."
35. "I will learn to see my child's behavior with fresh eyes."
36. "I choose to grow for myself and for my family."
37. "I will be a mindful parent."
38. "As best I can, I will consistently show my children love."
39. "My love is stronger than my anger."
40. "I will be careful not to do too much for my children so they can be independent."
41. "I will use my child's name for their positive behavior, not just their negative."
42. "I respect my child, no matter how they are acting."
43. "I will carry out my authority in a calm and calculated way."
44. "I will not rush my parenting."
45. "I will consciously prompt my child, not just tell them what to do."

46. "My words count, so I will choose them carefully."
47. "I will allow my child to give me feedback on how I'm doing as a parent."
48. "I will try not to control my child because I can't control them. I can only control myself."
49. "I will remember that hitting is not helping."
50. "I will make sure my child grows up knowing they are loved."
51. "I will remember I can't make my child be good, but I can facilitate good behavior."
52. "I will remember to cherish my children, no matter how they are acting."

Okay. That's a wrap. I think I've written the book I was meant to write.

Now, let's see what happens...

APPENDIX B

Conscious Parenting Posts by Category

BEHAVIOR THERAPY AND MANAGEMENT

- January 7, 9, 10, 13, 15, 18, 19, 20, 22, 24, 26
- February 4, 12, 21, 22, 28
- March 3, 4, 5, 9, 12, 13, 19, 23, 25
- April 10, 13, 14, 17, 20, 29
- May 27, 28, 30
- June 3, 6, 15, 19, 20, 21, 23, 24, 27
- July 10, 18, 19, 21, 25
- August 3, 12, 16, 19, 25, 30, 31
- September 5, 14, 20, 21, 24
- October 6, 10, 17, 22
- November 7, 11, 14, 20, 21, 26
- December 7, 15, 21, 28
- Why Not Try This? Pages: 24, 61, 65, 78, 84, 96, 114, 115
- Case Study: Page 129

CALMNESS AND STABILITY

- January 12, 17, 23
- February 6, 8, 13, 23
- March 5, 24
- April 8, 10, 18, 23
- May 12, 16, 21, 23
- June 12, 25
- July 5, 14
- August 17, 19, 28, 30
- September 6, 19, 20, 22, 26
- October 11, 17, 18, 31
- November 6, 11, 23
- December 2, 7, 16
- Why Not Try This: Pages: 24, 39, 77, 78, 86, 109
- Case Study: Page 132

CHILD PSYCHOLOGY

- January 1, 13, 16, 18, 20, 21, 22, 25
- February 15, 26
- March 7, 11, 15, 16, 22, 28
- April 3, 22
- May 1, 19
- June 13, 31
- July 8, 10
- August 4, 18, 23
- September 3, 8
- October 3, 4
- November 9, 21
- December 13, 23
- Why Not Try This: Pages 17, 39, 44, 61, 84, 109, 118, 135
- Case Study: Pages 60, 81,121, 132

- Psych 101: Pages 16, 27, 41, 55, 62, 69, 85, 90, 105, 106, 119, 124, 128, 130

COMMUNICATION AND UNDERSTANDING

- January 2, 11, 14, 26
- February 2, 9, 16, 17, 24, 26, 27, 29
- March 3, 10, 11, 17, 19, 20, 23, 29, 30
- April 1, 4, 14, 19, 21, 26
- May 2, 8, 9, 11, 15, 17, 19, 20, 22, 25, 27
- June 1, 14, 16, 22, 24, 28
- July 1, 10, 13, 24, 26, 27
- August 1, 10, 17, 23, 26, 30
- September 5, 9, 14, 22, 25, 27, 29
- October 9, 11, 13, 22, 28
- November 3, 21, 23
- December 2, 4, 10, 16, 18, 29
- Why Not Try This? Pages 35, 39, 82, 84, 100, 102, 105, 109, 122
- Case Study: Pages 14, 50, 95, 96, 121
- Psych 101: Pages 62, 69, 105, 106, 112, 119

CONSCIOUSNESS

- January 11, 21, 28
- February 5, 7, 10, 19
- March 6, 21, 24
- April 15, 30
- May 1, 5, 7, 13, 18, 23, 27
- June 3, 5, 9, 11, 18, 26
- July 13, 22, 30
- August 8, 17, 27
- September 10, 16, 19, 24

- October 1, 18
- November 2, 15, 17, 19, 26
- December 11, 20, 24, 29
- Why Not Try This? Pages 71, 83
- Case Study: Page 15
- Psych 101: Pages 112

EDUCATION AND SELF-DEVELOPMENT

- January 29, 30, 31
- February 2, 7, 23, 29
- March 1, 3, 4, 22
- April 1, 3, 8, 12,
- May 1, 7, 20, 26
- June 7, 8, 13, 14
- July 1, 8, 9, 11, 15, 19, 22, 29
- August 4, 14, 15, 18, 21, 22
- September 3, 4, 8, 9, 13
- October 4, 5, 8, 20, 23, 26
- November 2, 4, 6, 12, 16
- December 3, 6, 10, 15, 19, 20, 27, 31
- Why Not Try This? Pages 20, 30, 32, 39, 44, 53, 55, 58, 65, 82, 93, 96, 100, 102, 106, 109, 114, 123, 133, 134
- Case Study: Pages 60, 81, 132
- Psych 101: Pages 90, 130

EMPATHY AND SENSITIVITY

- January 3, 10, 13, 14, 26
- February 2, 4, 9, 11, 25
- March 3, 7, 20, 28
- April 1, 3, 6, 17, 24
- May 2, 5, 6, 29

- June 2, 4, 18, 26
- July 2, 8, 20, 23
- August 1, 7, 15, 26
- September 6, 13, 18, 20
- October 3, 8, 9, 19
- November 3, 13, 17, 18, 25, 29
- December 9, 12, 25, 28
- Why Not Try This? Page 122

GRACE AND FORGIVENESS

- January 3, 8
- February 1, 2, 6
- March 7. 8
- April 4, 7, 27
- May 2, 5, 8
- June 3, 9, 18
- July 5, 8, 17
- August 8, 23, 24
- September 11, 18, 22
- October 28, 29
- November 4, 18
- December 2, 4, 14
- Why Not Try This? Page 99
- Psych 101: Page 112

HOMELIFE:

- January 12, 17, 23, 25, 26, 27
- February 8, 25, 26, 27, 29
- March 6, 8, 11, 19, 24
- April 1, 4, 7, 11, 21
- May 4, 5, 8, 14

- June 2, 7, 8, 12
- July 16, 27, 28
- August 2, 10, 11, 13, 20, 21, 31
- September 1, 10, 12, 21, 25
- October 2, 12, 19, 23, 25
- November 1, 7, 8, 13, 19, 22, 28, 30
- December 6, 17, 21, 26
- Why Not Try This? Pages 53, 54, 61,105, 118, 123, 133, 135
- Case Study: 112

LOVE AND KINDNESS:

- January 2, 4, 5, 6, 8,10, 11
- February 4, 24
- March 18, 20
- April 7, 9, 11, 12, 16, 24, 25, 27
- May 4, 6, 10, 24, 29
- June 10, 23
- July 7, 9, 12, 20, 30
- August 5, 6, 13, 14, 20, 24, 28
- September 2, 11, 18
- October 14, 24, 29, 30
- November 1, 9, 15, 25, 2
- December 5, 17
- Why Not Try This? Pages 14, 54
- Psych 101: Page 128

NON-EMOTIONAL REASONING AND DETACHMENT:

- January 7, 12, 16, 28, 31
- February 7, 26
- March 15

- April 8, 25
- May 3
- June 25
- July 2, 12, 23, 27
- August 5, 22
- September 1, 6, 10, 13
- November 20
- December 3, 19
- Case Study: Page 50

POSITIVITY AND NEGATIVITY:

- January 3, 9, 10, 14, 15,
- February 5, 11
- March 2, 25, 28, 29, 31
- April 5, 13, 16, 17, 28, 29
- May 10, 28, 30
- June 15, 18, 27
- July 9, 11, 24
- August 3, 12, 25

So you may be thinking, who is this guy?

Fair question. I went to Hendrix College, where I received an above-average liberal arts education. My strategy in college was simple: take the classes I had to take (ho-hum), but then sign up for all the classes that sounded really interesting to me. At the end of my sophomore year, my guidance counselor asked me about the subject in which I intended to major. I had not given it a moment's thought! On a whim, I asked her which class subjects I had taken the most. She looked over the previous two years and said I had the most classes in philosophy, then religion, and then psychology. I asked her about job prospects in each field. She told me that if I majored in philosophy—and got my PhD—I could teach or write books. At that time, the idea of more education did not appeal to me. I had two more years of undergraduate classes, for Pete's sake! I had always been taken by spirituality and loved learning about world religions, but I could not believe I was, in any way, cut out to be a "man of the cloth." That left psychology. I enjoyed all of my psych classes, so why not? Two years later, I graduated with a BA in psychology and a minor in English, class of 1978. My inevitable encounter with the "Real World," for which everyone had been helping me prepare, had finally arrived…

Time to get to work! My first job was working with juvenile delinquents to help them become productive members of society. These guys ate my lunch! (I wouldn't begin to understand how to work with conduct disorders and sociopathy until much later.) The higher-ups at the re-entry program had mercy on me and moved me to Steppingstone, a shelter for runaway kids. These kids were sad, anxious, and had serious family problems, but most of them were open and ready to change. They wanted to both feel better and do better.

I worked at Steppingstone for two years and absolutely loved it. But, I began to realize I would make no real money with a bachelor's degree. Still, I knew I had found something I loved. So, I signed up for the graduate program in Counseling Psychology at the University of Central Arkansas, put in my two weeks' notice, and started waiting tables to make ends meet.

Looking back, I came to see graduate school as a hoop I had to jump through so that I could start my real education, which was actually working with troubled kids and their families. However, when I graduated, there were no jobs for master-level clinicians. Being extremely tired of waiting tables, I took a bachelor's level position at Rivendell, a long-term residential treatment facility for children and adolescents. I admit, at first, I was a little bummed not doing actual therapy, but slowly I began to see the position was most serendipitous. I got to work with children on the unit, eight hours a day, five days a week, implementing the behavioral program. Looking back, I realize this was the absolute best way to start my career—on the front line, seeing behavioral psychology in action and immersing myself in it. I know this one thing helped me so much more than sitting behind a desk and seeing children for one-hour therapy sessions twice a week.

The Rivendell behavioral program consisted of verbal cuing, rewards, and consequences. As a Floor Therapist, I clearly saw what worked—and what didn't—all through the eyes of a master-level clinician. I did eventually become a therapist and a Psychological Examiner. I took a short detour into some administrative positions but quickly discovered they were not for me. My passion is and has always been working with the kids and trying to help them and their families do better.

During this time, I married Lee Anne. After four years of couple-dom, we started a family when one would be correct to say, the real education began. I was older when we had Hannah, our first child. (In therapy, I sometimes tell young parents who lack confidence that I was 35 when I had my first child and I was "almost mature enough to pull it off"). For a second time, I found myself in a most serendipitous position. I had worked with emotionally and behaviorally disturbed children for five years, and here I was, having children of my own. As I watched Hannah and later Emily grow and develop, some interesting insights came to me, insights I would not have had without my psychological training and experience. I shared many of these in my first book, *Fingerpainting in Psych Class.*

I am pleased to say I am still married to LeeAnne. Hannah is an outpatient therapist specializing in children, teens, and young adults, while Emily is a transplant pharmacist working with patients so that transplanted organs are not rejected. (The older I get, the more I can see how their chosen careers could also be serendipitous. It's comforting to know there are close family members to help if I develop mental health issues or if one of my original parts wears out.)

After 10 years working at Rivendell, I decided to devote my time to keeping kids out of the hospital. My outpatient practice then began under the tutelage of Dr. Warren Seiler, a gifted child and adolescent psychiatrist and my greatest mentor. I am still working with children and still helping families. Looking back over the last 40+ years to the present, clearly, there are more and more kids (and parents) who need real help—help that works.

Thank you for checking out my book. More consciousness is not a pipe dream—it's available to anyone and everyone. These posts are snapshots of the big picture. If you would like to go in deeper, please consider my other books, which are listed below.

Welcome to the only quest that really matters—transcending the ego and reconnecting with our higher self. This will help not only with parenting but in every aspect of life. I hope to see you on the journey!

JAY MORGAN

Other Works

Fingerpainting In Psych Class—
Artfully applying Science to better work with children and teens.

The Little Book of Sutras—
Spiritual snacks for those on the road less traveled.

Join us on Facebook:
@consciousparentingnow

Acclaim for Jay Morgan's book, "Fingerpainting in Psych Class," artfully applying science, to better work with children and teens.

A Conscious mom writes: *"As a general rule, I don't like parenting books. They either make me feel like I'm doing something wrong, or they make me feel mad because I know I'm not doing anything wrong—even though I'm going against the author's specific recommendations. I am a big believer in trusting one's parental instincts and tailoring an approach that works for each unique child. But 'Fingerpainting' is one parenting book I like, and often recommend. It provides great information, sometimes in story form, along with practical techniques that really help parents deal with children and effectively address difficult family issues with insight and compassion."*

Irene writes, *"WONDERFUL, powerful book. I don't have enough words to describe how impressed I am with what I have found in this book. The many principles shared here were not new to me, yet the examples, practical application, tips, and real-life situations are helping me bridge theory and practice. The author's own journey and insight are most inspiring and thought-provoking. The book is filled with wisdom, kindness and good common sense. Highly recommended! I am a fan! :)"*

Acclaim for Jay Morgan's second book, "The Little Book of Sutras," spiritual snacks for those on the road less traveled.

M.J. writes: *"I stumbled upon Jay Morgan's 'EnlightenMeNow' Facebook page about a year or so ago, which features some excerpts from 'The Little Book of Sutras'. At the time, I was at a crossroads in my life and needed guidance to know where to begin to find the answers I sought. I found the simple sutras featured in this book life-changing once I began to apply them. With the help of this book and lots of conscious determination to rediscover my higher self, I am pleased to say that I am a much more content and centered person today. I highly recommend this book to anyone on a journey toward inner peace."*

The Road Less Traveled, by Scott Peck

The Power of Now, by Eckhart Tolle

Transforming the Difficult Child, by Howard Glasser and Rebecca Easley

The Anatomy of Peace, by the Arbinger Institute

The Outward Mindset, by the Arbinger Institution

Fingerpainting in Psych Class—Artfully applying science to better work with children and teens, by Jay Morgan

The Little Book of Sutras—Spiritual snacks for those on the road less traveled, by Jay Morgan

www.ingramcontent.com/pod-product-compliance
Lightning Source LLC
Chambersburg PA
CBHW071422150726
48000CB00001B/445